P9-CLN-942

Just Like Someone
Without Mental Illness
Only More So

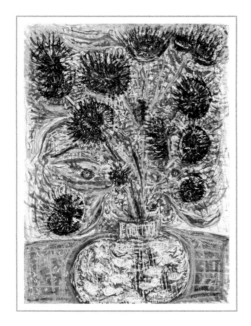

Flowers and Fish, 2005

(Painting by Mark Vonnegut)

Just Like Someone
Without Mental Illness
Only More So

A Memoir

Mark Vonnegut, M.D.

Delacorte Press
New York

Just Like Someone Without Mental Illness Only More So is a work of nonfiction. Some names and identifying details have been changed.

Published in the United States by Delacorte Press, an imprint of The Random House Publishing Group, a division of Random House, Inc., New York.

DELACORTE PRESS is a registered trademark of Random House, Inc., and the colophon is a trademark of Random House, Inc.

Library of Congress Cataloging-in-Publication Data

Vonnegut, Mark.
Just like someone without mental illness only more so: a memoir / Mark Vonnegut.
p. cm.
ISBN: 978-0-385-34379-4
1. Vonnegut, Mark. 2. Pediatricians—Massachusetts—Boston—Biography. 3. Schizophrenics—Massachusetts—Boston—Biography.
4. Children of celebrities—Massachusetts—Boston—Biography.
I. Title.
RJ43.V66A3 2010
618.92'8980092—dc22   2010009765
[B]

Printed in the United States of America on acid-free paper

www.bantamdell.com

987654321

First Edition

Book design by Virginia Norey

The other day I found the final version—along with several drafts—of the note below:

Dear Santa,

Can you please get me the large set of Pickett's Charge (soldiers, horses, cannons, fences, trees, and a hill)?

From Oliver

Living with a seven-year-old who asks Santa for a 470-piece Civil War battle replica play set is a great joy and privilege. Yesterday he asked me, "So what happened to the slaves after the Emancipation Proclamation?"

This book is dedicated to all seven-year-olds...and *their* seven-year-olds and *their* seven-year-olds and so forth and so on.

Contents

A Note on the Title

When I talk to the National Alliance on Mental Illness (NAMI) and other patient support groups, I take questions at the end. At one talk I was asked, "What's the difference between yourself and someone without mental illness?"

At another talk I was asked, "How do you make the voices be not so mean?"

I wish I knew.

Introduction

I've gotten used to it, but very little about my life has been likely. In my early twenties I stopped being able to eat or sleep. I heard voices, went up against locked doors, was given a lot of medication, and lost my confidence that going crazy was something that happened to other people. It would have made perfectly good sense for me not to have done well and maybe have ended up killing myself after x number of relapses. Everyone would have adjusted. But I recovered enough to be able to think about what I would have wanted to become if it wasn't for the sixties and mental illness. I wanted to be a doctor and applied to twenty medical schools. It was a round number.

It would have been utterly unremarkable for all twenty to have said no. That the one that said yes was Harvard is either a miracle or a very funny joke.

Luck and circumstances make us as different from who we might have been as cats are from dogs and birds are from bugs. There must be a point in paying attention to what goes on. My father's fame falls into the one-in-a-zillion category. Had I told someone after my first series of breaks that I might go to Harvard

Medical School, they would have upped my meds and canceled my dayroom privileges.

I've had the bad luck to get sick four times and the remarkable good luck to get better again each time. None of us are entirely well, and none of us are irrecoverably sick. At my best I have islands of being sick. At my worst I had islands of being well. Except for a reluctance to give up on myself there isn't anything I can claim credit for that helped me recover from my breaks. Even that doesn't count. You either have or don't have a reluctance to give up on yourself. It helps a lot if others don't give up on you. Had I been a little sicker a little longer or taken a little longer to get better, I never could have applied to, let alone gotten into, medical school. I managed to get well in the nick of time, by the skin of my teeth, needing every ounce of every resource I had.

And if you're lucky enough to survive going crazy and get back to the point where you can pass for normal, it builds a question into the rest of your life. You have to forgive people for wondering, "How all right can he be?"

After my fourth break, fourteen years after the first three, when everything was supposed to be okay because I had graduated from medical school and was a respected physician in the so-called real world but I fell apart anyway, my task was, once again, to get my sorry, sick, humiliated self back together as quickly as possible. Because if I didn't stand up and do a credible job of walking and talking, my license and job would have been up for grabs, and then how would I be able to tell if I was okay?

My psychotic episodes start out great. As a reward for diligence, patience, and the refusal to accept lesser gods, I am set free. We're all one, really and truly one, free at last, blissfully overwhelmed by God's boundless love. There's peace and universal brotherhood. There's no need to wait for the other shoe to drop.

And then, a few weeks later, ten or twenty pounds lighter, I'm foggily embarrassed in a cold world with things that need doing, like figuring out if I can still be a doctor and how to explain mental illness to my young children.

✳

There were crazy people in my family, but I had figured out good and sound reasons why I wouldn't go that way. I was stronger than that. But then there were three breaks in quick succession in 1971. I was diagnosed as suffering from schizophrenia. With the publication of the third edition of the *Diagnostic and Statistical Manual of Mental Disorder* (*DSM III*) in 1980, the diagnosis of schizophrenia was made more standard and required continual symptoms for at least five years. What I had and have is more consistent with what is now called bipolar disorder, which used to be called manic depression. The name change was an effort to get away from the stigma around the diagnosis of manic depression. Good luck.

Until we come up with an unequivocal blood test or the equivalent, we're all blowing smoke and don't know if what we call schizophrenia and bipolar disorder are one disorder or a dozen.

Break number four, in 1985, came as a complete surprise and taught me once and for all that what I think is and isn't going to happen doesn't count for much. My friends and family and psychiatrist all think I'm doing well and won't go crazy again, and I appreciate their optimism.

※

In the middle of break number one, I made a lot of promises. When I promised to try to remember to tell the truth, it seemed to help.

It's now been almost twenty-five years since my last break. It was a matter of faith that I could go to medical school and do a pediatric internship and residency and that it would turn out okay. I've had a good run as a pediatrician. I'm happily married and have three healthy sons, but I'll never fully shake the feeling that I'm being tracked by the voices and a parallel psychotic life.

"You didn't really think you could lose us, did you?"

※

PRACTICE, PRACTICE, PRACTICE

Most adults have forgotten what they had to do to survive childhood.

I've spent most of my professional life thinking about how to improve and safeguard the health of children, studying what others have figured out about their major and minor ailments and trying to cram this knowledge into the day-to-day work of a pediatric practice. It's been a privilege to watch my patients and their parents closely to see what works and what doesn't work.

If you had told me ten years ago that today my patients would routinely have to wait eight-plus hours in an emergency room to get not-very-good care, that every day my staff and I would spend hours arguing and doing paperwork to have my patients get basic medications, that there would be six-month waits to see specialists, again with the blizzard of paperwork, and that psychiatry would be essentially unavailable for children, especially ones with mental health problems, I would have asked what backward third-world country we were living in.

When I open the office on Sundays to see acutely sick kids, it takes my wife at least twice as long to check a patient in and verify insurance information as it takes me to diagnose and treat the problem. There's an excellent chance even with all that checking that the insurer will find a way to not pay. Medical care has become a lot of crust and precious little pie.

PHYSICAL SIGNS

If I know their parents and siblings and cousins, I can look at someone with Down syndrome and see who he would have been if not for the split-second failure of chromosome 21 to separate from its copy. The disease is like a transparency. Separating out who and what a person is and what a disease is doing is much easier with acute illnesses and if you know the patient. In an otherwise well child, lobar pneumonia sticks out like a sore thumb. The longer a disease has to become part of a person, the harder it is to tease out. My job is to be an optimist and see people as potentially better than they are, and their problems as possibly removable overlays, as in "He's a really great kid but he has a drug problem." It's also my job to tell the truth when there are things that aren't going to get better.

I want my young hands back, the ones that don't shake so much. The tremor that I've lived with my whole life is worse because I take lithium and drink coffee and am older. It's my tremor more than being sixty-two or anything else that lets me know I won't be able to do what I do now forever. It's embarrassing to reach a stethoscope forward and have it shake against the patient and have to use two hands to steady the damn thing.

I've learned how to examine children without making them cry. I know how to quiet crying babies. I know that most blood tests, most referrals, and most medications are unnecessary. I don't want my patients and parents taken advantage of. It is not a matter of great importance whether or not a given child has an ear infection. She will likely get better with or without help. But it is important that the person diagnosing the ear infection be doing so competently and honestly.

There's an unfortunate hustle built into medical care, which favors doing things over not doing things. Most medical care is delivered by a provider who doesn't know the patient and will never see him again. Doing things is more comfortable than not doing things. Doctors have much more at stake in their relationships with insurers and business managers than in their relationships with patients.

I worry more about patients now than I did when I was younger. Now a sick-looking child with a sky-high fever or a funky heart murmur I didn't hear before doubles my pulse and makes me a little nauseous. I am confident that I can sink my teeth into any pediatric problem and hold on till the damn thing gives up, but that's different from feeling like Clint Eastwood, the way I used to. Maybe I was unnaturally calm when I was younger and I'm paying for it now. A calmness debt.

It would help if I was a step back from the action, maybe in a tweed coat or corduroy jacket. At sixty-plus I didn't expect to still be wrestling the terrified, swabbing the throats, being peed and thrown up on, and giving shots. I expected to have taken up a more gentlemanly position.

✳

There are now a million templates and decision trees and practice guidelines, the underlying intent of which is to make medical care idiot-proof. Anyone with half a brain can check off boxes, and the pattern of the checked boxes tells you what the patient has and what to do about it. The problem with templates and clinical guidelines is that patients without asthma get crammed into asthma templates. Providers are rewarded financially and otherwise for small lies that make the templates and guidelines come out right.

Medicine can't be made idiot-proof because idiots will always find a way to start or end up in the wrong place. The doctor gets credit for a 99214 ICD-9 493.10 and will be paid for such, with a bonus payment for asthma management under the quality-improvement asthma initiative. Unfortunately asthma might or might not have had much to do with what was bothering the patient. It's amazing how well you can get paid for doing a crummy job.

There is something very pure—and easy to screw up—about trying to do the right thing without doing harm. Medical care has become a minefield of incentives that distort that purity. In some settings, revenues can be dramatically "enhanced" by ordering X-rays and tests or even doing unnecessary surgery. In other settings, providers can be penalized for ordering tests or making referrals. A doctor whose productivity incentives demand that he see four to six patients an hour delivers different care from one setting her own pace. A doctor under time pressure is more likely to come up with a quick diagnosis and treatment. Checklists and productivity goals become proxies for care. The proxies are what you get paid for, and the care goes to hell.

I want needlepoints on my wall that read:

> *The less you have wrong with you, the longer*
> *it will take me to find it*
>
> *It's faster and much more profitable to do a test*
> *than to explain why it's not necessary*
>
> *Beware of what you get paid for*

If medical care makes people poor and dependent, it's no different from cancer, whooping cough, or malaria.

Sometimes for me to get a stethoscope to the chest or push a tongue down or to move the earwax out of the way to see the eardrum is an epic struggle like the one described in Jack London's story "To Build a Fire." Sometimes I'm saving the world. Sometimes I'm just trying to see the damn eardrum. Sometimes by trying to see the damn eardrum I'm saving the world.

Of course I'm trying to save the world. What else would a bipolar manic-depressive hippie with a BA in religion practicing primary-care pediatrics be up to? If the saving-the-world stuff doesn't work out, I have steady work and a decent income.

Just Like Someone
Without Mental Illness
Only More So

Young Jane and Kurt with me, circa 1948

(Vonnegut family photo)

chapter 1

A Brief Family History

It's good to have a sixth gear, but watch out for
the seventh one. If you think too well outside the box,
you might find yourself in a little room without much in it.

The arts are not extracurricular.

One hundred thirty-nine years ago, my great-grandfather Bernard Vonnegut, fifteen years old, described as less physically robust than his two older brothers, probably asthmatic, started crying while doing inventory at the family hardware store. When his parents asked what was wrong, he said he didn't know but he thought he wanted to be an artist.

"I don't want to sell nails," he sobbed.

Maybe his parents should have beaten him for being ungrateful, but they wanted their son to be happy and the business was successful enough that they could hire someone else to do inventory. He became an apprentice stonecutter and then went to Europe to study art and architecture. He designed many buildings in Indianapolis that still stand today. He drew beautifully, made sculptures and furniture. He was also happily married and had three children, one of whom was Kurt senior, my grandfather, who was known as "Doc" and who also became an architect. Doc could also draw and paint and make furniture. He made wonderful chessboards, one of which he gave to me when I was nine.

When he was sixty, Doc was pulled over for not stopping at a stop sign. The cop was astonished to notice that his driver's license had expired twenty years earlier.

"So shoot me," said Doc.

At the end of his life, which had included financial ruin in the Great Depression, his wife's barbiturate addiction and death by overdose, and then his own lung cancer, Doc said, "It was enough to have been a unicorn." What he meant was that he got to do art. It was magic to him that his hands and mind got to make wonderful things, that he didn't have to be just another goat or horse.

When I worked on the Harvard Medical School admissions committee, artistic achievements were referred to as "extras." The arts are not extra.

If my great-grandfather Bernard Vonnegut hadn't started crying while doing inventory at Vonnegut Hardware and hadn't told his parents that he wanted to be an artist instead of selling nails and if his parents hadn't figured out how to help him make that happen, there are many buildings in and around Indianapolis that wouldn't have gotten built. Kurt senior wouldn't have created paintings or furniture or carvings or stained glass. And Kurt junior, if he existed at all, would have been just another guy with PTSD—no stories, no novels, no paintings. And I, if I existed at all, would have been just another broken young man without a clue how to get up off the floor.

Art is lunging forward without certainty about where you are going or how to get there, being open to and dependent on what luck, the paint, the typo, the dissonance, give you. Without art you're stuck with yourself as you are and life as you think life is.

✳

Craziness also runs in the family. I can trace manic depression back several generations. We have episodes of hearing voices, delusions, hyper-religiosity, and periods of not being able to eat or sleep. These episodes are remarkably similar across generations and between individuals. It's like an apocalyptic disintegration sequence that might be useful if the world really is ending, but if the world is not ending, you just end up in a nuthouse. If we're lucky enough to get better, we have to deal with people who seem unaware of our heroism and who treat us as if we are just mentally ill.

My great-grandfather on my mother's side drank to keep the voices away and ended up the town drunk in the middle of Indiana. My maternal grandmother wrote textbooks on teaching Greek and Latin and had several bouts of illness that resulted in long hospitalizations. When my mother, Jane, was in college the family resources were exhausted after my grandmother spent over two years in a private hospital. With great shame and embarrassment her husband transferred her to a state hospital, where she became well enough to go home a few weeks later. She remained mostly well and never had to be hospitalized again, but she had spent roughly seven years of my mother's childhood institutionalized.

There was no acknowledgment of or conversation about my grandmother's illness either between my mother and her father or my mother and her brother, who would also be in and out of hospitals most of his life. He emerged normal enough to marry three times in his fifties and sixties, hold a job as a librarian, and be the Indiana State senior Ping-Pong champion.

This same maternal grandmother warned my mother not to marry my father because she was convinced there was mental instability in the Vonnegut family. My father's mother, a barbiturate addict who didn't come out of her room let alone the house for weeks at a time, told my father to stay away from my mother because there was mental illness in the Cox family. My father's mother famously (some say it was an accident, but does it really make a difference?) overdosed and killed herself on Mother's Day. Barbiturates had been prescribed to my grandmother as a wonderful new nonaddictive medicine for headaches and insomnia.

If you want to pick out the people who go crazy from time to time in my family, find the ones in the photos who look ten or more years younger than they actually are. Maybe it's because we laugh and cry a lot and have a hard time figuring out what to do next. It keeps the facial muscles toned up.

It's the agitation and the need to do something about the voices that get you into trouble. If you could just lie there and watch it all go by like a movie, there would be no problem. My mother, who was radiant, young, and beautiful even as she lay dying, heard voices and saw visions, but she always managed to make friends with them and was much too charming to hospitalize even at her craziest.

If you don't have flights of ideas, why bother to think at all? I don't see how people without loose associations and flights of ideas get much done.

The reason creativity and craziness go together is that if you're just plain crazy without being able to sing or dance or write good poems, no one is going to want to have babies with you. Your genes will fall by the wayside. Who but a brazen crazy person would go one-on-one with blank paper or canvas armed with nothing but ideas?

The psychotic state is a destructive process. A fire can't burn that brightly without melting circuits. Making allowances for individual tolerances and intensity and duration of the breaks, complete functional recovery becomes increasingly unlikely much beyond about eight or nine breaks. Fixed delusions, fears, loss of flexibility, loss of concrete thinking, and low stress tolerance make relationships, jobs, and family next to impossible and then impossible. The biggest risk factor in determining whether or not you have a nineteenth psychotic episode is having had the eighteenth.

Life for the unwell is discontinuous and unpredictable. Things just come out of nowhere. People try but mostly do a lousy job of taking care of you.

It Is Good, 2009

(Painting by Mark Vonnegut)

chapter 2

Raised by Wolves

*The biggest gift of being unambiguously mentally ill
is the time I've saved myself trying to be normal.*

I grew up on Cape Cod. The vine forest a couple hundred yards
from our house was two and a half acres of trees being wrestled
down and killed by honeysuckle vines and wild grapes. There
were flesh-tearing bull briars throughout the lower level. There
was one path that got you into the vine forest and out the other
side, where the abandoned apple orchard and old foundation
were. I could hit that wall of green at a full run with a knife and
fishing rod and disappear. I doubt anyone could have followed
me even if they saw where I went in. I built wolf dens in the vine
forest next to the pond and imagined I could live there if I had
to. My mother was storing canned goods and water in the
crawlspace under the house in case of nuclear war.

I was mostly left alone to figure things out. If I'd been raised by
wolves, I would have known a little less, but not much less,
about how normal people did things. My notions about how to

brush my teeth, what could be left out of the refrigerator for how long, and where knives and forks and spoons went were odd. Having been raised by wolves would have given me an excuse. But I just had beautiful, slightly broken, self-absorbed parents like a lot of other people. One of the things I couldn't figure out was why I had such lousy handwriting and why I couldn't spell.

I fought at school almost every day during grades three, four, and five. I won most fights and was never mad or emotional about it. It was just the way it was.

What I liked best about the stories of children raised by wolves was that everyone snuggled in together in a nice warm den. And then there was the part when the people find you and teach you how to talk and wear clothes.

✳

I had a rich, full, and seemingly complete world before I knew much. My father tried to explain about sex to me when I said "Fuck you" after a chess game. I said it in a perfectly cordial way; it was something I had heard and was trying to use in a sentence. Kurt told me something about going to the bathroom in the same toilet that sounded highly improbable.

When I knocked a few dozen bricks out of a partitioning half-wall under the barn and started making a bomb shelter, it was meant as a present to my father. It was something I thought he would have gotten around to eventually. I was surprised that he wasn't more pleased. He thought that knocking those bricks out made it more likely that the already wobbly barn would fall over.

At this time in my life, my father was a proudly antisocial

man who spent most of his time at a typewriter, reflecting negatively on his neighbors and society, throwing in things like "Goddamn it, you've got to be kind." The emphasis was on the *Goddamn it.* He was proud of the fact that I had no friends.

Later, I could never get used to him dressing nicely and talking nicely and smoothly navigating social situations with people he had taught me to hate. I thought, and still think, he taught me to play chess partly to make sure I didn't fit in with the locals my age.

When I was ten I told my mother I wanted to kill myself. I was failing at school and sports and fighting every day and had been studying poisons. My mother told me that bright young idealistic people like myself were going to save the world. It was a successful play for time. Before I killed myself I should at least join forces with all the other suicidal ten-year-olds and give saving the world a try. When the sixties came around and there didn't seem to be any adult plans worth much, I thought my mother's solution was coming to pass. Making the world a place worth saving was up to the outcasts. Who would have guessed in the fifties that there would be such a thing as hippies?

When I had three psychotic breaks in three months and I didn't think getting better was possible, my childhood looked particularly dark and dismal. Now, not so bad.

I liked to take my fishing rod and my bike and go through the woods looking for hidden ponds, which I imagined had never been fished before except maybe by Indians a long time ago. Dense rings of brambles and underbrush protected the ponds and fish.

One bright sunny August afternoon I was cruising the dirt

back roads that ran along the spine of the Cape and went straight instead of taking the usual left to Hathaway's Pond. Twenty yards ahead I found myself at a dead end, facing a chain-link fence. At the top there was a two-foot-wide chain-link lip slanted back away from me at a forty-five-degree angle. I threw my bike over the fence. I expected Hathaway's or some other pond to be more or less ahead of me.

Hathaway's was one of the town's bigger ponds and one of the few that had anything like a sandy beach. Toward the end of my childhood, the powers that be decided to poison the pond so that they could get rid of the pickerel and bass and horned pout and turtles and stock it with trout. I had bad dreams about grown-ups killing all the pickerel in Hathaway's Pond—it was death on an unimaginable scale. It would have broken my heart to see the fish I had been trying to catch strewn around dead.

Why were trout better than pickerel and horned pout?

I stumbled up onto a divided four-lane highway. I couldn't have been any more surprised if I had found China. It had to be over a hundred degrees up there, at least twenty degrees hotter than it had been on the sandy, pine-shaded dirt road. A maintenance crew was spraying thick, hot oil on the shoulder, probably to keep the weeds down. Turning left would have brought me to the Barnstable Road overpass and familiarity within a hundred yards or less, but I chose to go right. Maybe it was to go with the traffic instead of having to face it.

The oil was awful. I checked the chain-link fence every so often, hoping for a break. I tried to ride my bike, but it was all gummed up with oil. I had to push it. Maybe I should have left it there and come back for it. I was going through the spit-warm water in my canteen quickly. Vacationers streamed off the Cape past the quaint ten-year-old boy with a fishing rod bent over his bike pushing it through the oil and dirt in the hundred-plus-degree heat. No one in his right mind would have stopped to let this dirty little boy and his bike into their car. I existed without an explanation. I was out of water.

I pushed my gummed-up bike along the burning shoulder of a divided limited-access highway for 2.7 miles before I saw Howard Johnson's and the Route 132 exit. The Howard Johnson's was the only place we went out to eat as a family, and that had only happened once. It didn't go well. I ordered a 3-D burger, a two-patty triple-decker precursor to the Big Mac. I can't remember exactly what went wrong, but I might have been stuttering or laughing or chewing gum when the waitress asked me what I wanted, or maybe it was something one of my sisters did. We left under a cloud. My father went stiff and red whenever there was a hint of public humiliation.

Pushing my gummed-up bike was by far the hardest thing I had ever had to do. Swimming home across the pond worrying about snapping turtles after my boat sank moved into second place. I was relieved when I made it to the exit and the shoulder wasn't oiled. I was able to ride the bike a bit, pop into the woods, and follow the path to the house of my only friend, Carl, where we cleaned most of the oil off the bike and myself with kerosene. Carl didn't ask any questions, and I didn't try to explain anything.

Twenty years later I would take care of two brothers at the Shriner Burn Institute who caught fire when they were washing tar off their bikes with kerosene somewhere in Texas. One of them had no hands or face left.

I rode my bike home, and it was like nothing had happened.

Once I was oriented again it was hard to believe that I really hadn't known where I was, and I would have been embarrassed to admit it.

When I was twelve years old Kurt took me with him to a science-fiction writers' convention in New Milford, Pennsylvania, at a camp on the Delaware River. It was just the two of us. A mean-looking judge ran the motel and diner where we stayed.

"I'd hate to come up in front of him," said Kurt, who'd gotten some virus and was throwing up bile on the side of the road. "Will you look at that? It just keeps coming. There's nothing down there, and it keeps coming. Will you look at that?"

There was nowhere else to look.

There was a woman with scraggly, greasy, gray-black hair at the conference who said, "Get that kid out of here," talking about me. I guess she had something important to say to her fellow science-fiction writers that she didn't want a twelve-year-old to hear. I got up and went down to the Delaware River to fish.

I cast my red-and-white spoon lure out toward a twenty-five- to thirty-foot-long serpent, but it was much too far out. My twelve-pound test line would have just snapped anyway. I knew right away that I could never tell anybody about this and wondered if maybe Kurt and some of the other writers, maybe the one with the damp, scraggly hair, could have or would have set something like this up to see what a twelve-year-old boy would make of a twenty-five- to thirty-foot-long serpent swimming down the Delaware. I fixed them by saying nothing.

We also met a guy who owned a waterfall and made a living showing it to people.

✳

When Kurt tried to sell Saabs, he usually did the test drive with the prospective customer in the passenger seat. I tried to tell him to not go around corners so fast, especially if the customers were middle-aged or older, but he thought it was the best way to explain front-wheel drive. Some of them were shaken and green. He didn't sell a lot of cars.

"Maybe you should just let them drive," I suggested.

✳

When I was ten Kurt asked if he could borrow the three hundred dollars I had saved up from my paper route. Ten years later he went from being poor to being famous and rich in the blink of an eye. No one, except him, ever quite got used to it. He felt that rightful order was being restored.

I grew up thinking everything would be perfect if we just had a little more money. Instead the money just blew everything apart. Humans will money themselves to death the same way some dogs and fish will eat themselves to death. If the rich were truly so productive and useful, they wouldn't have so many hired-gun talking heads with talking points, foundations, and institutes. Eventually most kings come to believe in the divine right of kings.

Once he was famous, people gathered around my father like hungry guppies around a piece of bread. There was never enough Kurt to go around.

Toward the end of his life he told me that he was glad he had been able to restore the family fortune. It surprised me that such a thing mattered to him. It didn't seem like an important enough goal for him to worry about. But he had grown up living in a nice house with a cook who taught him how to read, in a nice neighborhood with an architect father doing what he liked and being well paid for it. All that had ended abruptly with the Depression and his parents losing their savings to a stock scam.

The thing I've always loved about my troubled paternal grandmother—who I imagine as not yet troubled back then—was that when informed by her husband that they were broke she said, "Okay. Let's spend the summer in Europe."

And they did.

✳

At some point in my childhood, my father gave us all code names. He was Boraseesee. My mother was Mullerstay. I was Kindo. If we were ever trapped or captured and wanted to let one another know that it was really us, we could use these names. It was a long shot, but when I was locked up, Kindo tried hard as hell to get word out to Boraseesee and Mullerstay.

We all want to believe that we're in a sheltered workshop with grown-ups nearby.

When my father came to see me the first time I went crazy, I was sure it wasn't him. My father was taller and thinner than the stand-in they sent, and he used a fake name to order a cab. I played along, figuring the trip to see me was too dangerous for Kurt to be able to make it. Crossing time zones wasn't the half of it.

I was twenty-one when *Slaughterhouse-Five* was published. I mostly didn't live at home anymore, so it was like watching from afar when the money hit. My sisters grew up as the children of a famous writer. I did not.

The people who lived around us on the Cape had more money than we did. What my father saw as a brief period of wrongful relative poverty was my childhood, to which I was firmly attached and of which I was and remain intensely proud.

After the Coming of the Orphans.
I am on the far right.

(Vonnegut family photo)

chapter 3

The Coming of the Orphans

When I was a boy
There was reason to believe
That people did good things for good reasons.

Why would a couple in their early thirties with only two children and another on the way buy a sixteen-room house? Living in a house so much bigger than a family with three kids needed became a part of my mother's religion. We had all the standard rooms plus a porch big enough to play Ping-Pong on, a study for my father, a study for my mother, seven bedrooms, and a secret stairway leading to a room we didn't know what to call. There was a spacious attic with windows looking out over a pond and the marsh and a barn to fix up someday. It was a glorious magical house because my mother made it so, at least partly to force her nuttiness and the world to coexist.

The year before my aunt and uncle died my mother would get up at night and stockpile blankets and food in the attic. When my father asked her what she was doing she replied that the refugees were coming. She was getting messages from license plates and traffic lights. *The refugees are coming.*

My father and the local GP were on the verge of hospitalizing her when the demands of making a home for my orphaned cousins more or less snapped her out of it. Later, I asked my mother if she didn't think the refugee stuff and getting messages from license plates and traffic lights was a little nutty, and she pointed out that it was around the time of the Hungarian uprising and there were lots of refugees. When the orphans/ refugees came she decided that messages from license plates and blinking lights were more or less reliable.

Whenever we went somewhere that involved leaving the house for more than a few hours, my mother would pretend to have forgotten something and run back into the house. It would only take a minute or so, but there were prayers and rituals that had to be done to ensure that the house wouldn't burn down while we were gone. Certain light switches had to be left in the up or down position.

Years later, when I complained to her about the voices, she said, "Why don't you just go along with them?" Her voices never got nasty the way they do eventually for most people.

My Uncle Jim was on the only commuter train to ever go off an open drawbridge into Newark Bay. This was in 1958, and the conductor, who also died, was either asleep or already dead from a heart attack when the train ran several stop signals and went into the bay on the way into New York's Pennsylvania Station. Forty-eight people died, including my uncle. His body wasn't found for a week, so there was at least a hope that he was knocked out or dazed or trapped somewhere, maybe washed up on an island. His wife, Allie, my father's sister, died of cancer a day and a half after the train went off the bridge.

My father heard about the train wreck on the radio. It wasn't the usual train Jim took, but when Kurt called his office and Jim wasn't in, Kurt figured it was possible that Jim had been on the train that had gone into the bay. Jane drove him to the airport, and he headed down to New Jersey.

When my cousins got home from school, my father was there. They had no idea about the train accident. It still wasn't known for sure that their father was on that train. Their mother died the next day not knowing whether or not her husband was dead. My Uncle Jim could go up and down stairs walking on his hands. No one could believe he couldn't get out of a sinking train.

The four boys were suddenly orphans. Only the oldest, fourteen-year-old Jim, had known his mother was seriously ill. Steve was eleven. Tiger (Kurt) was eight years old, and Boo (Peter) was only eighteen months. My father packed them up with their two dogs and a pet rabbit, Phee Phee, who bit, and they all came to live with us in Barnstable.

My mother and father, at the ripe old age of thirty-five, struggling financially (ten years prior to *Slaughterhouse-Five*), took on four more children, two dogs, and a rabbit. Whatever else good or bad my parents did or didn't do with the rest of their lives, that was absolutely the right thing to do.

There was no way to ask for a replay or argue or complain about Allie and Jim dying. You just had to keep going and do the best you could.

Taking in the orphans turned my parents into instant heroes. Kurt and Jane were looked on with awe and admiration, and everyone wanted to do something to help. It was all over the papers. We fixed up the house some, and my mother became "Aunt Jane" to me and everyone else.

There was no even cursory social-service-type investigation into whether or not this was a family that could or should take care of four orphaned children.

The youngest cousin orphan, Boo, was still in diapers, and he cried and banged his head all the time. He could bounce the crib from one side of the room to the other with ten or twelve head butts. My youngest sister was only a year older than he was and tried to kill him. Jim, the oldest, had had adjustment and social-ization issues before his parents died. Shortly after arriving in Barnstable he packed a neighbor's front door with black powder and lit a fuse to see what would happen. The door blew up.

Our house was huge but had a tiny kitchen and one and a half marginal bathrooms. The Adams relatives, my Uncle Jim's family, had money but no space for the orphans, so they gave us a new kitchen and laundry room and an upstairs bathroom, but what my mother really needed was help with cleaning and laun-dry and cooking.

Somehow my mother found Ruby. Ruby was a wonderful baker, especially of pecan sticky buns. They really were very very good, but there was a lot else that needed doing and my mother had a hard time telling people what she needed from them if it wasn't something they were already inclined to do. I have inherited this from her, along with her gift for visions and voices. So the helping out Ruby could do with the cleaning, cooking, and laundry for the two adults and seven children in a friendly but crumbly two-hundred-plus-year-old house was fit in around the baking of the sticky buns.

My mother asked Ruby if she could make the sticky buns once a week or so and asked us to please not eat them all so Ruby would think that we had had enough, but I could no more not eat all the sticky buns there were than I could fly. Luckily

Ruby had a sister and some cousins who were more inclined to cleaning and laundry, so it was worked out that Ruby came once a week to do dinner and sticky buns, and various combinations of her sister and her cousins helped out with the other stuff.

Fifteen years later, at age fifty, my mother tried to get a master's degree in social work. When she was told that she would have to repeat the first year of a two-year social work program if she wanted to continue, I explained to her that maybe she was being counseled out of the field.

Jane had an utter and complete lack of distance from people with problems. As long as it was all in a book and hypothetical she was okay, but as soon as she met flesh-and-blood people with real problems, she thought long and hard about what could be done and could never escape the idea that she, Jane, should move in with the family and straighten things out and maybe call up Ruby and her cousins to see if they could help.

Before the orphans came, my mother had a friend or two but was mostly having a hard time fitting in. My parents were over-educated midwestern liberals a long way from home with hopes and ambitions that would have perplexed and mystified their neighbors. Most Cape Codders had grown up on the Cape like their parents and their parents before them. They had quiet jobs and inherited a little money they didn't talk about. The women probably didn't like that Jane was pretty and our house was run-down. We were not into team sports. We were doing nothing for property values. It was not at all clear what my father did for a living. He was a tall, dark-eyed, gawky, hunched-over guy you wouldn't just go up to and get to know or talk to about baseball.

The year before the orphans came, some neighbors down the street asked my mother if they could take me to a football game.

It must have been at Barnstable High. I went and was fascinated but didn't have even a little idea about what was going on.

✳

Average looked good to me growing up.

There are a bunch of things my father said that I could, as long as I was very sure he wasn't around, mimic with close to perfect tone.

"Do you want to be average?"

"Take your friends and shove them."

"Not world-class."

I took it as a compliment—maybe I was capable of being world-class if I worked a little harder. It just meant my father had high standards and wasn't going to gush about every little thing his children did.

One of my sisters, defending a report card, said that C was average.

"Do you want to be average? Sandy's average," said my father, maligning our sweet, part sheepdog mongrel. This was my sister Nanny, who I thought for a while might have been average like me. My mother took me aside one day and told me that Nanny had taken some test at school and that she was very smart. I imagined her IQ vanishing up into the stratosphere. "Gee, that's great," I said.

I couldn't help noticing that when you got A's, grades didn't matter.

✳

Most of the children I take care of travel. Just about everyone goes to Disney or some version of Florida, or at least they go on long drives to see relatives.

We took one trip to New York; the buildings were tall and it snowed. And one trip to New Hampshire; the car stalled and almost fell off Mount Washington.

"Uncle K, are we going to die?" asked Tiger, who was nine years old.

✳

My father was not average. He was a better writer than Hemingway or Fitzgerald, but no one knew it yet, which was why we didn't have any money. The pressure to make money made it so he couldn't write, so he had to try to sell cars, which he was very bad at. You couldn't do just anything if you were a genius.

My mother wasn't average. She was Phi Beta Kappa and had worked for the CIA. She knew my father was going to be famous and it was all going to be worth it. She knew about lots of things before they happened, like my cousins coming to live with us and who was calling on the phone before there was such a thing as caller ID. She would have hated caller ID. No one would have been surprised that she knew who was calling.

My cousins weren't average. They were orphans who eventually all got to be over six feet tall. My sister Edie could draw like Leonardo da Vinci and seemed never to have worked at being able to do that. My mother said Edie's hands looked very old. It was like this little girl was going to be born and Leonardo's hands were sewn onto her at the last moment to some great purpose.

I learned how to play chess young and could beat just about everyone I played, but it was mainly a party trick I didn't fully understand. Being a good chess player in Barnstable didn't mean much. I didn't see any real advantage in being smart. I worried that bigger, less smart people might figure out what

I was thinking and beat the crap out of me. I honestly couldn't understand why so many people played chess so poorly.

My father thought it was fine that I didn't have friends or play sports. I didn't know what to think about it. Friendships and sports were like spelling and handwriting—things that were supposed to be easy and that were easy for most people but mysteriously inaccessible to me.

I didn't want to beat my father in chess because it put him in a lousy mood. So I'd have a pretty good attack going and then try to back off. But I couldn't make a completely stupid move because he played well enough to catch me at that. I'd sometimes end up with two or three good attacks going and he'd all of a sudden see it and realize that he was utterly cooked. He could throw the board pretty far. I think it was a joke, but my sisters and cousins took it seriously enough to urge me to find a way to lose. Surely I could figure out how to throw a game or two, but it was more complicated than that. I was at least a little afraid to play him until he was about sixty, when his game and mood around chess improved quite a bit.

✳

Once, my parents went out to dinner and on the way home they went to King's to pick up a mop and some lightbulbs. My father noticed that the music being played over the PA was a waltz. He asked my mother to dance, and they waltzed in the aisle. Before the song was over the music changed to a fox trot, which they handled no problem. The music changed again. Fast, slow, rumba, tango, whatever, my parents danced to everything that was thrown at them. After fifteen minutes of trying to stump the dancers, whoever was watching them through the shoplifting surveillance system gave up and the PA went silent. My parents paid for the mop and the lightbulbs and came home. When they walked through the door they were laughing so hard they were crying.

✳

I had a lot of hope, and in the end I was right, that good things would come out of having my cousins come live with us. Steve was just three months older than me, tall, blond, blue-eyed, and destined to become captain of the football, basketball, and baseball teams, as well as class president. So I learned how to do sports and say hi to people. It was Steve who discovered that I was so nearsighted as to be legally blind. I found out later that when he was pitching in Little League, Steve would go into the woods before games and throw up.

The cousins were a breath of fresh air. I was glad for the company. In my own way I became socialized enough to talk to girls on the phone and play middle linebacker and keep playing even when I had a broken wrist.

When I was eleven my mother sat down on the edge of my bed and explained to me the difference between *egoist* and *egotist*. I didn't have the faintest idea what she was talking about. I resolved to remember it in case it turned out to be important.

There seemed to be a lot of winking going on when I was growing up. I assumed there must be some good reason why people couldn't just come out and say things.

When I was sixteen I met Lonnie Crews, a serious kid who wore a black leather jacket and told me he thought he might die young and that once you died you couldn't learn anymore. I started reading a lot and asking people about what and who

I should read. I didn't want to be stuck with a junior high education. Things started sticking, and what I knew became something I could do something about.

✳

Introverts almost never cause me trouble and are usually much better at what they do than extroverts. Extroverts are too busy slapping one another on the back, team building, and making fun of introverts to get much done. Extroverts are amazed and baffled by how much some introverts get done and assume that they, the extroverts, are somehow actually responsible.

I can pass for normal most of the time, but I understand perfectly why some of my autistic patients scream and flap their arms—it's to frighten off extroverts. It was on purpose that I didn't stick out, but I never thought I had a choice. Even when I had a full beard, hair halfway down my back, and was headed out to British Columbia to start a commune, I figured that anyone born and raised the way I was would be doing the same thing; I thought I was white bread.

When I didn't eat or sleep for two weeks, lost twenty-five pounds, and came to in a nuthouse with labels like *schizophrenic* and *paranoid* being thrown around, that was the first thing in my life that seemed not white bread. The downside of not sticking out, not being a high-wire act, was that I didn't have any excuses. The other thing was that I probably would never be loved.

After the orphans came, I tried to be as little trouble as possible. Breathing a little less air and taking up a little less space seemed like the least I could do. I moved into an attic space over the kitchen that you couldn't stand up in and told myself and everyone else that I liked it, another wolf den. I tried to breathe next to no air and leave next to no footprints.

A psychotic break is the exact opposite of not taking up much space and being as little trouble as possible.

"Mark's in the hospital."

It hurt my feelings that no one, during my first series of breaks, in the seventies, or the last one, in the eighties, ever asked, "What kind of hospital?"

I've found it helps a lot to get older. Now when honking cars start sounding like my name or other things happen that could be the voices warming up, I'm not thrilled or terrified. "I've got a lot going on," I say. "You'll have to wait your turn."

If I wasn't optimistic, who was?

(Vonnegut family photo)

chapter 4

Hippie

To live outside the law you must be honest.
—Bob Dylan

I went through junior high, high school, prep school, and college like an unremarkable person. I tried to say things I remembered Steve saying in similar social situations to see if they would work for me. I did a little bit well at sports and then decided sports were unimportant.

I always had a job and I always worked hard. Whether it was mowing lawns or clearing brush or loading trucks, I liked to sweat and get into a rhythm where I could think. I wasn't sure what thinking was good for, but I was resolved to pay attention to what went through my mind just in case. If I had a job, like pumping gas, where there were lulls in the work, I always had a book to read and argue with.

I took up painting and felt lucky and not particularly responsible when the paintings came out well. It wasn't like I knew how I did it or thought I could do it again or that I thought painting was important. I did well on standardized tests, but everyone knew how inauthentic they were. I loved playing music but didn't think I was good enough or had the balls to become a full-bore musician. People said I wrote well. I liked learning about history and literature. I gave up math after nearly flunking calculus in college. I took learning seriously and was probably perfectly prepared for something. Sometimes I thought I was a genius. Sometimes I thought I was a coward and a phony. I got along pretty well with just about anybody. I was serious about being serious and wasn't about to adopt just any old notion of what that might mean.

My hair got longer and longer. I grew a full beard right after high school and looked as much like Jesus Christ as possible. I was serious about being a hippie, and being a good hippie seemed like a job right up my alley and maybe something I could do better than Steve or Jim or Tiger or my father.

There were drugs involved but not nearly as much as movies about hippies would have you believe. It seemed like almost everyone smoked some pot, but it wasn't an every-day or even every-week sort of thing. Even then, we knew there was something wrong with people who smoked pot every day. A great many hippies, myself included, managed to get through college without doing psychedelics. Cocaine and heroin didn't become commonplace until the seventies and eighties. In general, we saw drugs as a possibly useful part of discovery and growth. We looked down on people who were just trying to get blasted.

I acquired a sophisticated appreciation for a few beers now and then, and an occasional bottle of bourbon. Somewhere in there I became a good cook and added knowledge of wine to the things to which I could introduce my friends.

At Swarthmore I majored in religion with the idea of going

to divinity school and then maybe the Unitarian ministry, where I would be a comforter of the sick and disadvantaged but mostly a really good professional arguer who argued against war and materialism.

Our parents and teachers were demoralized by the war and how imperfect America, the world's last best hope, was turning out. After the Ohio National Guard loaded up with live ammunition and killed four students at Kent State, no one knew what to expect or where things were going. Mainstream jobs and careers seemed beside the point, and how long was corporate America going to last anyhow? I and a dozen or so friends at college came up with the idea of starting a commune in British Columbia. We thought about it and talked about it and bought books about it and talked some more, and it seemed more and more like the best thing—maybe the only thing—to do. Parents, professors, and psychiatrists we consulted all seemed to think it was a reasonable idea. They had nothing better to offer.

We were going to take a shot at making of this world a paradise or know the reason why such a thing couldn't be done.

So in 1971, along with a bunch of similarly idealistic, long-haired hippies, I traveled across the continent and managed to buy eighty acres twelve miles back from the coast. We camped out while cutting down lumber and building a shelter. It wasn't as hard as we thought it was going to be. We managed to keep ourselves warm, entertained, and well fed. There were lots of people doing similar things in similar places up and down the coast and back East. Whether or not Western civilization was about to collapse, it had to be good news that setting up independent alternative communities was doable. We were proving it was possible to achieve escape velocity.

We ground our own flour, ate tons of wild fruit, caught a two-pound trout every cast, and bought some goats from a woman named Cougar Nancy. I shot a few grouse with my .22 from back home. We were almost self-supporting. We had living expenses down to sixteen cents per person per day, and we had enough money left over after buying the place to keep going for at least another year. Then maybe we'd have to draw straws to see who had to work at the pulp-and-paper mill to support the rest of us. We'd take turns. Maybe we could gather and sell smoked trout and some of the abundant wild fruit and chanterelle mushrooms and fiddlehead ferns.

"Wild is better than organic—don't trust food that needs people" was going to be our motto.

Building buildings, cutting firewood, hunting, gathering, cooking, cleaning up—there was no lack of things to do. We were setting up a beachhead for all our friends and family who were for the moment stuck back East or in the cities. We were ready for the storm.

Most of us were in close touch with our parents. It's a myth that hippies on communes like ours were at war with their families. Parents would have had to be nuts to look at the world as it was then and tell their children to clean up, get a job, find a nice mate, have some children, and stop complaining. It was like we were mainstream, cover-of-*Newsweek* cultural warriors, and then all of a sudden we were dropped like a bad joke, silly dead-end hippies.

There were Vietnam vets on communes in British Columbia. They were more than welcome. If there was any spitting on troops done, it was by hired provocateurs desperate to make sure that pacifism didn't gain a foothold and cripple our ability to defend ourselves.

Celebrating the beauty and fullness of life, we had a house and food and a winter's worth of firewood cut. Maybe all the things we had been told had to be the way they were didn't really have to be that way. We, who had been the best and the brightest, the National Merit scholars, and the students of the week and captains of the teams... were setting up a way of being that could survive without poisoning everything. We believed that we had been given the chance to be heroic. It was like *Mission: Impossible,* where the tape self-destructs and the powers that be deny all knowledge of our mission and say we were just a bunch of silly hippies.

There was a wonderful feeling of having enough and being *enough.* Right before I stopped being able to eat or sleep and the voices started, I knew that I was enough. Where I was, what I did, who I was with, and what they did was all enough. It was true and simple, and I was about to get the living crap kicked out of me for figuring it out.

I could feel my thick Old Testament hair lift in a good wind. Life had its bumps, like my parents splitting up and an unfaithful girlfriend and most of the firewood I had cut and split getting rained on instead of drying out, but it didn't seem like anything I couldn't handle. I was like a Russian peasant who's been beaten and left for dead in a ditch by the tsar's henchmen after they burn the family hovel. I pulled myself to my knees and saw the beautiful green of the first leaves of spring, and then...

zap—snap—crackle—pop

Like 5 to 10 percent of humans, I go crazy. I'm twenty-three years old.

There are overwhelmingly rich, beautiful feelings of universal brotherhood. All of a sudden I can't eat or sleep. . . . I'm hearing voices. . . . I'm not sure who I am or where I am. . . . Maybe I caused an earthquake. . . . Maybe my father killed himself. . . . Life is over.

Then it turns out that I'm in a psychiatric hospital, which is not good but is better than what I thought was happening.

When I was asked if I was hearing voices—"Is the radio or TV talking directly to you? Can others read your mind?"—it was a relief to finally be talking to someone who knew what was going on.

It was probably because my mind was just feeding me back material I had put into it, but it felt like I was able to survive psychosis and maybe save the world because I had read the novels I had read and knew what I knew.

"I'll try Russian Literature for four hundred."

"Early Christianity for the whole ball of wax."

There were times when I was crazy when I was perfectly all right. I'd be locked in a windowless room with an observation hole in the door wrapped in a sheet and think, "Why can't someone come talk to me now?" Whenever I was okay, I wanted to make the most of it, since I now knew what being not okay was.

It's explained to me and my friends and family that I have schizophrenia, but I'm young and healthy and did well prior to getting sick, so there's a chance I'll get better. I'm treated with major drugs; electroconvulsive therapy, affectionately known as shock treatment; and massive doses of vitamins that don't do much beyond underline the idea that what I have is a medical problem.

The commune we started in British Columbia was not a failure because I went crazy, and it didn't last forever. Nature turned out to be more merciful and bountiful than it might have been. We were independent, we were mostly well, we were mostly happy. We did at least as well as most people in their early twenties.

Among the things I grew up thinking about mental illness was that it was caused by other people or society treating you badly. I also knew that once people were broken they didn't usually get better and that the ones least likely to get better were paranoid schizophrenics, which is what I seemed to be. Paranoids are able to incorporate anything that happens into their worldview, which works against them.

I swear I was trying to be cooperative, but it didn't look that way from the outside.

In a month or so, with a lot of medication, I'm well enough to leave the hospital. So I do, but without any medication. Within two weeks I'm back to hearing voices and not eating or sleeping and being a bizarre frightened frightening soul whose friends take him to the hospital in Powell River. Lots of people there seem to wish me well, but they are all speaking in code. The Royal Canadian Mounties bundle me up and fly me back to Vancouver in a little Cessna and drive me in a police ambulance to Hollywood Hospital. *I really didn't know I was supposed to keep taking that medicine. No one made that clear to me. Really.*

Hollywood Hospital? If I'm supposed to calm down and take this seriously and stop connecting dots like I'm on a quiz show, the least they could have done is *not* drag me off to some supposed hospital, supposedly named Hollywood.

At that time how a schizophrenic was going to do was thought to depend on how well he had done before—pre-morbid adjustment. When I was doing well it seemed like my childhood and parents hadn't been so bad. If I took a turn for the worse, so did my past. Sometimes the commune and being a hippie worked in my favor but usually not. Somewhere in there they cut my hair and shaved off my beard to show me how much I looked like Hitler. A doctor later apologized for that and told me there would be no more forced haircuts or shaves.

I'm getting better again, taking medication, doing my very best to be a good patient, but then out of the blue, the chain-link fence that surrounds the hospital pulls me toward it, wraps around me, and is going to crush me. Everything is all twisting turning roller-coaster topsy-turvy, too much meaning, voices, too much to do when what I'm doing is my best to stand still. Maybe my childhood wasn't so good. Maybe my parents did things wrong. Maybe I'm not going to get better.

Was it my fault I didn't have a better pre-morbid adjustment?

At some point in there I try to tell my father that I'm feeling better, and he says that he wouldn't nominate me as Mr. Mental Health quite yet. I want to ask him if he is in the running or just one of the judges.

Years later, Kurt was hospitalized for smoke inhalation after he was in a fire probably caused by falling asleep smoking. I went into the William Randolph Hearst Burn Center in New York and said, "Hi, Dad. It's Mr. Mental Health. How's the best-looking guy on the burn unit doing?"

There came a fateful day I needed cigarettes and walked a couple hundred yards down the hill from the hospital to buy tobacco and rolling papers from a convenience store. I think we had permission to leave the hospital grounds. I was with a heroin addict who was trying to be my friend and had earlier fought the orderlies twice on my behalf, once when I was being taken upstairs for shock treatment. I tried to tell him not to bother, that things were playing out the way they should.

I have money on account at the hospital canteen/snack bar. They have plenty of cigarettes, but they aren't my cigarettes. Sportsman tobacco in a clear plastic jar is what I want, if they have it, and rolling papers. The hauntingly beautiful girl behind the counter looks so like an old girlfriend she might really be her. I'm fingering my money in my pocket and don't see any Sportsman tobacco. I can't be the first nut from the hospital up on the hill to wander into her shop. My friend the heroin addict looks like a mental patient for sure.

Was there a protective force field or special air at the hospital that I wasn't yet ready to be without and maybe whoever gave us permission to walk down the hill didn't know about it? I ask for Sportsman tobacco in a clear plastic jar and rolling papers, and the beautiful girl smiles and finds exactly what I'm looking for and I have the correct change.

Back out on the sidewalk, the hill back up to the hospital is steep, almost a cliff, and the six blocks looks like a million miles. There are crosswalks and traffic lights. The pack-hunting forces of evil have sunk a million micro grappling hooks and tiny arrows into the muscles of my legs and lower back. I'm following my addict friend, who seems to think this is just another routine walk. He moves his right foot. I move my right foot.

If I just give up and lie down on the sidewalk, which seems like the sensible thing to do, help of some sort will come. I'm never doing this again. The cigarettes in the canteen are fine.

Ever since then, whether I'm dissecting corpses or getting through long gory operations that aren't going well or taking hours-long board-certification exams, I remember that hill and figure if I made it back up, I can do anything.

We got to the hospital and checked ourselves back in. It was like we were never gone. I had my tobacco and rolling papers and somehow a turning point had been reached and I was going to be okay. Had I freaked out in the store or just lain down on the sidewalk, maybe the world would have become one where I relapse and relapse and relapse and can't get back to a world where I can learn and hold a job and be okay.

Hollywood Hospital was the last hospital treating alcoholics with LSD. The alcoholics had much better rooms than I did. They had curtains and rugs. I needed to hallucinate and talk to God a little less, and they were supposed to hallucinate and talk to God a little more. I needed a little more bondage of self. They needed a little less.

An alcoholic named Wally tells me I'm not in charge anymore. He says I did a good job and everyone is grateful. I can relax and take care of myself. I'm much relieved.

I talked with Lincoln and Twain and Dostoyevsky and played saxophone with Coltrane. Van Gogh wanted to paint some more and was glad my hands were willing and available. Maybe it was all in my head, but where else is there for anything to be? As the person who bargained God down from nuclear cataclysm to a relatively mild earthquake and stopped Kurt Vonnegut from killing himself, and got to meet all those guys, it was a hard thing to come back to earth and be just a regular mental patient.

When I left Hollywood Hospital, I looked like hell, weighed 127 pounds, walked with a shuffle because of the meds, and didn't always react to things at just the right moment, but in there somewhere was a kid who had been tried by fire who didn't worry anymore about being white bread or a coward.

Self-portrait, circa 1972

(Drawing by Mark Vonnegut)

One of the original author photos for
The Eden Express

(Photo by Peter Vandermark)

chapter 5

Retooling

There's nothing more likely about a giraffe or a kangaroo
or a warthog than a unicorn, but unicorns don't exist
and the others do.

When I came back to the Cape, a million years ago now in
1972, Carl, the guy who had helped me wash the tar and oil off
my bike when I was ten, gave me a job watering lawns and car-
rying rocks for him. I was a slower-moving, much lighter,
slightly haunted, sort of clean-shaven version of my former self.
After they had shaved my beard at the hospital I grew it back,
and then I shaved it off myself when I got back to the Cape. I
felt naked. My fingers missed having something to play with.

"The beard made me look heavier," I explained when people
didn't recognize me at first and did a double take. I was on Thorazine, from which I would be weaned a little at a time if I did
well. There had been shock treatment. It was all a little vague. I
worried about saying something wrong. Maybe if I relapsed,
being crazy and all, I'd be the last to know. It was like I was in
a logrolling contest suddenly finding myself in the cold water

looking up at the lumberjacks on top of the logs wondering how they walked around like that.

Somewhere in there my father left my mother and the Cape for good and went to live in New York. It was somehow about writing. He said that taking on the orphans, his sister's children, had cost him his wife and peace and had been hard on me and made it hard for him to write. It didn't ring remotely true then or now. He was just a guy who couldn't blend in and had to keep making up different stories about it.

In the ten years prior to the orphans he had published one novel and a bunch of short stories without coming close to making a living at it. The roughly ten years disrupted by orphans produced *The Sirens of Titan; Mother Night; Cat's Cradle; God Bless You, Mr. Rosewater; Welcome to the Monkey House;* and *Slaughterhouse-Five.* Not so bad.

As soon as I got out of the hospital after my first series of breaks I started writing about what had happened to me. Writing is very hard mostly because until you try to write something down, it's easy to fool yourself into believing you understand things. Writing is terrible for vanity and self-delusion. It wasn't therapy as much as trying to tell a story that took me by surprise, plus there weren't a lot of people beating down my door with alternative plans for what I should be doing.

I imagined neighbors saying, "I think he's writing in there."

"Whatever. As long as there's no screaming or broken glass, he can do whatever he wants."

In the middle of the illness I had promised to try to remember and tell the truth. One of the first pieces of mail I received after getting out of the hospital was from a magazine wanting to pub-lish a story I didn't remember writing, which I took as a helpful, possibly divine hint about what the hell I might be good for.

I thought the fact that people could get well from serious mental illness was good news and worth writing about. It was good news that it was more about biochemistry and neuro-transmitters. There should be no shame or blame. They were ill-nesses like other illnesses.

It crossed my mind that if I was able to tell the story well enough to get it published and it sold well, I might make some money and it might be the end of shame and blame and stigma-tization. The medical model would reign supreme. Unequivocal diagnostic tests would be available shortly. Medications without side effects would come along a little later, and mental illness would become a thing of the past.

It was not impossible that an accurate understanding of mental illness would lead to world peace and universal prosper-ity. Without writers fooling themselves about what their books might accomplish there would be no books at all.

And further, by these, my son, be admonished: of making many books there *is* no end; and much study is a weariness of the flesh. —*Ecclesiastes 12:12 (King James Version)*

Once a week and then every two weeks and then once a month, I drove up to Boston to see my old friend Dr. Kirk. Be-fore, I had been doing due diligence, checking out whether it was crazy to try to set up a commune in British Columbia. It seemed odd that a psychiatrist working at Harvard in the sixties and seventies had a crew cut and looked like a Marine. His ap-pearance was a testament to my open-mindedness. My Harvard crew-cut psychiatrist had said that my plans to set up a commune in British Columbia were just fine and, in fact, probably what he himself would be doing if he was my age. Now I was seeing him for permission to take a little less Thorazine. Our relationship had range.

"How are you sleeping? Eating? Any voices? Ideas of reference?"

"Not me, boss."

"Let's go down to fifty milligrams three times a day."

Today, if I was lucky, I'd see a case supervisor monthly and maybe a psychopharmacology nurse every three months. Clinical guidelines would mandate that I be on antipsychotics for at least five years. The medication I was on would be determined by who paid for lunch and what deal was cut between my health insurer and the pharmaceutical industry.

It didn't seem all that special at the time, but the fact that a doctor and I were left alone to figure out what was best for me was a lifesaving miracle.

My father had been teaching creative writing at Harvard and had seen Dr. Kirk a few times, which is how I got to see him the first time around. My now impeccably dressed in Brooks Brothers clothing father, increasingly recognized and recognizable with his multi-book contract and growing bank account, told me in a letter that he enjoyed the Harvard experience because it gave him a chance to know people who were *at home in the world.*

Kurt the pained loner seemed to be gone, but was he really winking at me like it wasn't for real as he went to fancy places with fancy people? Was he really a representative of loners and misfits? Where was I at home? Would I be called upon to rule a small but very nice planet in some faraway galaxy once my apprenticeship on Earth was done?

From the team owner's box, where I sat with my father, I watched Pelé play soccer and score a goal with a bicycle kick over his head for the New York Cosmos. After the game I went to the locker room and got to see Pelé's feet. They were the widest, most amazing feet I've ever seen. I tried not to stare. I almost went to a cocktail party given by a game-show host. Were my father and I playing out some hysterically funny joke we couldn't talk about?

✳

The landscaping went well. I got a job substitute teaching at Barnstable High. That went well. I wrote a short article that got published.

I started painting again. The paintings were much lighter, mostly landscapes. I found that I liked watercolors better than oils. People actually liked my watercolors enough to buy them. I loved painting but I never felt like I was talented the way my sisters and my father were. Art came easily to them. They were graceful. My paintings were more peaceful than theirs, but painting for me will always be like trying to get up out of a tar pit while I'm fighting off Africanized killer bees.

Someone, maybe me, asks me what I would have liked to have done if it hadn't been for the sixties and all that and being mentally ill. I thought back to when I was nine or ten.

I should have been a doctor.

Part of getting better from being crazy included the realization that my life might be a lot longer than I had thought and that I probably wasn't going to get out of anything by having the world end or Western civilization collapse.

It was too bad I was twenty-five, hadn't taken the right courses, and had this mental health history. I had a *mental health history,* the way other people might have a suitcase.

I wondered how I'd do taking math and science courses again. It seemed like my brain was back and working well, maybe even better than it had been for a while. I thought I had stopped doing math and science because they were so German and responsible for so much death and destruction.

I should have been a doctor.

When I started taking premed classes at UMass Boston, I was thrilled to find that I could do math and science again.

My illness became a compass of sorts. I could ask myself whether something was leading me away from or closer to being crazy. There was less of the "six of this, half dozen of that" that had made up so much of life.

Marijuana seemed to have been working hand in glove with the damn illness and trying to do me in, so I stopped that without regret or difficulty. Part of what saved my life was my strong reluctance to part with money. I tried cocaine once and liked how chatty it made me, but I wasn't about to part with hundreds of dollars just to be chatty.

If you take good care of any disease by eating well, sleeping well, being aware of your health, consciously wanting to be well, not smoking, et cetera, you are doing all the same things you should be doing anyway, but somehow having a disease makes them easier to do. A human without a disease is like a ship without a rudder.

I cleaned up my diet, avoided sugar and caffeine, got regular exercise, and took medication as prescribed and vitamin B12 shots once a month. Being normal with a vengeance was a big step up from being mentally ill, but it wasn't without its problems. As soon as someone who has been crazy can pass for normal, he is offered a witness relocation program with a new diagnosis and a new childhood if necessary. Everyone needs reassurance that the beast has been contained. If you're going to go nuts over and over, why bother to get an education, a job, or a date for Saturday night?

I had a number of notes to self about voodoo, ESP, and other forms of belief in things unseen that seemed related to the voices and ideas of reference. These things were harmless for others but not so good for me. I'd had my fill, and then some, of "Wow."

Having a not entirely reasonable expectation that things will go well turns out to be exactly the sort of delusion that increases your chances for success in this world, be it getting into medical school or whatever. If in fact you are skating on thin ice, the last thing you want to do is slow down and think about it. Once I made it through the process and was actually admitted to medical school, my unreasonable expectation that things would go well became retroactively reasonable.

I bought some Brooks Brothers clothes. I regained the twenty pounds I'd lost and then some. I had a mustache for a while and then ended up clean-shaven. I looked younger than I was. There was a chip on my shoulder the size of Montana, but nobody noticed. Why had such a nice guy like me been so rudely put upon and interrupted?

I had three more articles published. I was running and lifting weights. I had a girlfriend. Someone wanted to publish my book. I enrolled at Harvard Medical School. I was a god-damned panzer division. I'll never know if a less disciplined, less vigilant, less muscular me would have done as well. I was burning the candle at too many ends and getting away with it.

I should have been a doctor.

✳

Note to self: Being Kurt's son, being an ex–mental patient, get-ting into Harvard, having written a book, and being a doctor are all things that in and of themselves do not make a life. If you lean on them too hard, you'll find that there's not much there. But if you add up enough things that aren't in and of themselves enough, it almost starts to add up to something. . . .

Painted by Kurt over the dining room mantel
in Barnstable, circa 1957

(Vonnegut family photo)

Pickup game

(Photo by Barb Vonnegut)

chapter 6

Bow Wow Boogie

The older we get, the better we were.
—United States Marine Corps motto

The Bow Wow Boogie was what we ended up calling our twenty-seven-inning softball marathon that took place the first weekend in August every year for thirty years. Just about everyone on the other team had gone to Harvard, but they wanted to be called the Boston Massacre. One summer in Cambridge they had made themselves into a softball team that was beating teams from the local Boston and Cambridge bars. Their captain had spent his summers in Barnstable and had beaten me for the under-sixteen Barnstable Yacht Club tennis championship, which was as close as I ever got to winning something in organized sports. He brought his team down for a weekend on the Cape and asked Steve, my cousin/brother/orphan, if he could get a team together so they could have someone to practice against. So Steve gathered a bunch of locals, including me. The baseball gods smiled on us and not them that day, and we won. Whenever we wanted to bother them we called them *Harvard*.

When I went to Harvard Medical School, some of my team-mates jokingly asked if I'd have to change sides. I was and am anything but ashamed of getting into and going to Harvard, but I found myself shuffling and explaining unnecessarily that it was the only medical school that took me, which was true. It confuses people who didn't go to Harvard when you try to avoid mentioning it or qualify it. And since you don't have to do it with people who did go there, all the shucking and jiving you do has to be mostly for yourself.

The other day a patient told me that he had gotten into what was a very good college. "It's not Harvard," he said.

"Harvard's not Harvard either," I answered.

For the first Bow Wow Boogie I was just off Thorazine and there was no thought that Harvard would be a part of my life except as a place my father had once taught. The Harvard guys were on average a few years younger than we were, they were better athletes, they aged better and won more series than we did. They hit better, ran faster, and made fewer errors, but baseball is a funny game and we had our wonderful moments and days that were all the more tasty because they expected to win and got so pissed when they didn't. We loved when they whined and snarled at one another.

We looked forward to the game all year, and when it was over we looked back on it remembering and talking about key plays, great catches, big hits. Everybody ran hard, threw hard, swung hard, and played hard, every play, every game. There was nothing *soft* about it. We were storing up things to make us feel good about ourselves for the rest of the year. It was my chance, and one I'm very grateful for, to make up for having gypped myself out of sports when I was younger.

I started out playing second base but switched over to catcher when a rational fear of hard-hit ground balls took hold of me and wouldn't let go. Catching was hard too. I dreaded having to block the plate and catch the ball when runners churned around third base and headed for home. It cost me the use of my left hand for two months and a minor permanent deformity when two bones in my left hand snapped like pencils. I would have given anything to have held on to the ball, but I dropped it and the run scored. Even when I knew for sure that the hand was broken—it was swollen and misshapen—I splinted it and coached first base and went to the hospital later, after the softball was over.

Toward the end it was like there was a sniper in the woods. Because the signal to lunge left or right and how hard was based on how strong and flexible you used to be and what you used to weigh, things tended to snap on the first step and the unfortunate player gave a yelp, grabbed a knee, and fell down.

It seemed like one year I could throw accurately and the next it was anyone's guess where the ball would go. I had been walking around with the false idea that if I caught a ball and threw it, I could control where it would go. The Yankees used to have a second baseman like that.

Once, toward the end, we let some of our eighteen- and nineteen-year-old sons play in the Bow Wow Boogie. It was horrible how beautifully they could run and throw.

When I was still young and the ball still went where I thought it would, I drank a lot at the postgame party and woke up at 2 A.M. at a green light and wondered how long and for how many green lights I'd been sitting there. I'd heard that blackouts were a sign of alcoholism but figured what they meant was blackouts when something bad happened. They should have said that rather than make normal people like me worry.

A few years before we quit the annual softball ritual, Vinny, the Harvard shortstop, was found dead in his rooming house, sitting in a chair dressed in a sport coat, next to an unopened six-pack. He died without bothering to fall over. We scattered his ashes at home plate the following August. As a medical student, one of the things I noticed about death was how little else happened. The patient who just died lies there quietly and everyone else stops rushing around trying to do something about it.

Vinny, like several of the Harvard softball players, had been good enough at sports to be recruited by several colleges. He had been the fastest, smartest, best-coordinated kid his small town had produced in a decade or so. His romance and charm lay in how well he did with what might have been and how gracefully he accepted what was. What Vinny was not graceful about or accepting of was making errors. He'd yell and swear and throw his glove and pick it up and throw it again. You could be sure that more errors were on the way. Up until Vinny made that first error, his demeanor and play were effortless, calm, and efficient. We spent considerable time trying to get Vinny to make an error as early in the first game as possible.

Trying to play sports as if you were twenty-something when you are fifty-something causes pain and suffering. Bones that years earlier would have flexed, shatter. Fractures that would have healed perfectly in six weeks take twelve and are never quite right. Tendonitis only gets better quickly if you are young. My cousin Steve needs his shoulders replaced and wonders if he should do both at once or one at a time.

I was expecting a slower decline.

I didn't play much baseball as a child. Part of the reason was I couldn't see the ball. For years I had gone up to the blackboard to read and copy questions. I didn't wonder why no one else did that. None of my teachers seemed to think it was unusual. I also had far and away the worst handwriting and spelling in the class. Needing to get up to read the board was just one more thing about me that was a little off. Closer up I could see well enough to read and did well on standardized tests.

I got to be almost fourteen before I was diagnosed as having 20/300 vision. My mother asked why I hadn't complained about things being blurry.

"Blurry compared to what?"

By the time I could see, Little League was done. In the sixties, aggression and competition were somehow implicated as root causes of war and misery and I was left high and dry as a pretty good athlete who loved trying to win whatever game was at hand. With the Bow Wow Boogie, it was a wonderful blessing to play softball every year with these guys who had been the Little League and high school stars. And if I came across a pickup game where they needed an extra player, I whacked the hell out of the ball and could play even more beautifully than I did in August. I don't think I ever made an error or hit less than .600 in a pickup game. I have never anywhere run across people in their fifties who insist on playing twenty-seven innings of softball in midday August heat.

I can also make game-ending jump shots when I'm playing basketball playground pickup games with strangers but not if I'm playing with people I know.

At the age of thirty-nine, three months sober, recovering from what will hopefully be my last psychotic break and hospitalization, I threw out a runner at third to preserve the tie in the top of the ninth and then got the game-winning hit in the bottom of the ninth with two outs and two strikes. I felt like complete crap that day and honestly don't know how I did either thing.

At Vinny's memorial service someone told me about watching him play football. I imagined a halfback so quick and strong he didn't really need blockers. And he was gracious and kind to younger kids and kids who weren't athletes.

What could be more contingent-dependent and improbable than the individual human?

Vinny quit Harvard midway through his second semester when he was accused of plagiarism. Everyone I've talked to was quite sure he hadn't plagiarized, but honor was involved and Vinny preferred quitting school, full scholarship and all, to defending himself. He was a reliable and valued worker, but after Harvard he never did anything, more than barely, briefly, a step above a menial job.

I've lived long enough now that if I condense time and look back at people I grew up with who have died, it looks like a minute or so of Antietam. There's not that much difference between leukemia, heart disease, flying into mountains, and bullets whizzing through the air. Maybe, because so few of my friends have been armed at the time of their death, it's more like soft-shelled newly hatched sea turtles heading for the water and being eaten by hungry gulls.

＊

Poem for Vinny

Your heart attack will not be what you expect
You will not have crushing chest pain
or pain radiating to your jaw or left arm
You will not have shortness of breath
They will not get you to the hospital just in time
You will not resolve to take better care of yourself
Quit smoking
Eat better
Take up yoga or kickboxing.

Earnest young man

(Vonnegut family photo)

chapter 7

Medical School

Science is a way of trying not to fool yourself.
—Richard P. Feynman

What we hope to get out of taking care of patients is a glimpse of a transcendent moment.

I believed that I was a bright enough, hardworking, idealistic kid who was good at math and science, who, if it hadn't been for Vietnam and the sixties and mental illness . . . if I hadn't been called upon to save too tough a world at too tender an age . . . maybe I should have been a doctor.

It was not reasonable for a twenty-eight-year-old with a 1.8 undergraduate math and science grade-point average, recently off heavy meds, to think he might be able to go to medical school, but there's something about manic depression that, if you're lucky, gives you a contagious optimism. I believed I should be a doctor, and people who met me back then, especially if they were interviewing me, came to think so too. Sooner or later a medical school had to admit someone six years off the beaten track, with three psychotic breaks and a 1.8 undergraduate math and science GPA. Maybe I'd be the guy.

✳

By the time I actually applied to medical school, I had put together two and a half years of straight A's at UMass Boston and had published a few articles in *Harper's* and *The Village Voice*. And I was working on a book that I thought was going well. Attitude was creating reality.

When I applied to medical school, no one asked me if I thought I was going to go crazy again. It was a more polite time. The questions I was asked were vague enough that I could have gotten out of talking about mental illness altogether, but how and why I came to be applying to medical school at the advanced age of twenty-eight didn't make much sense without it. My grades at Swarthmore weren't very good; my MCAT scores were good, but a ton of applicants had good MCAT scores. My only real distinction and accomplishment was having published a few articles, and they were about mental illness. "Why I Want to Bite R. D. Laing" was a seminal piece of work. Without being mentally ill, I was just another overaged, mediocre applicant. I had to project some strength that would make up for the fact that I'd have six years' less time to take care of patients than most applicants.

Somehow, some way, the insightful, providentially wise admissions committee of the day offered me a place in the Harvard Medical School class of '79. I was three years off of Thorazine. It had been almost four years exactly since I was hospitalized. Getting into medical school tied up my having been mentally ill with a big red bow.

He went crazy. He's the son of Godzilla.
Yeah, but he went to medical school.
Which one?

﹡

Harvard Medical School is five white-marble buildings surrounding a quadrangle of grass and walks. When the building in the Back Bay down near Mass General became too small, Harvard sent a delegation with plans to talk with Cornelius Vanderbilt, who looked the plans over and reportedly wrote out a $13 million check on the spot, saying, "Good meeting you, gentlemen. I believe that should cover it." So they named the dorm, which is also built out of white marble, after him. Vanderbilt Hall.

Seen from Longwood Avenue, Building A looks a lot like the Parthenon. There aren't any other buildings in the neighborhood that look like the Parthenon. There's a tree off to the side that was grown from a cutting from the tree on the island of Kos under which Hippocrates taught his students. Hippocrates gave us the famous oath that contains the admonition "First, do no harm."

The quadrangle was built in 1906. There were no antibiotics then. Surgery had to be very quick and was as likely to kill you as cure you. Keeping germs out of the surgical field was a novel idea. There were 155 medical schools in the United States, most of which were run for profit by one or two doctors, like trade schools. There were no admission requirements. If your family could pay, you could be a doctor. Doctors were taught and trained without being exposed to patients or science. The chances of any given patient being helped by any given doctor were slim. Most were peddling snake oil of one sort or another. The Flexner report, published in 1910, sought to improve medical care by making sure medical schools had reasonable admission requirements and were associated with universities and that medical education stressed the scientific method and empirical observation of patients. One of the things that stressing science and empiricism did was to democratize medical care and make innovation possible. In European medicine, medical students didn't have any exposure to patients; things were done a certain way because they had always been done that way, and all the various committees and academies and practice guidelines said they should be done that way. So the forces of innovation won, and American medicine became the best in the world, and all that white marble was trying to get us to be the best we could be.

After you've promised to "do no harm" and to honestly do your best to ascertain what is true, the rest is just details.

Science was the only way we could avoid fooling ourselves about what helped and what didn't. Doctors were supposed to act like battlefield medics, identifying and addressing pain, suffering, and disability. I believed that once you had a medical school education, especially a Harvard Medical School education, doing *good* was just a matter of showing up.

I liked all the white marble, but it can be hard to live with. The five buildings facing the quad appear to be not quite part of this world. They have wings that stretch and branch out into labs and foundations and institutes and hospitals and on and on into the so-called *real world,* but it's all connected to the white-marble hole.

My Harvard Medical School advisor had a recurring nightmare. He'd wake up in a cold sweat saying to himself, "This really is the best place."

There was and always will be a million miles between what my classmates and I wanted to do and what we would end up doing. We at Harvard and Harvard's teaching hospitals were the light and the way. All you had to do was ask us. It has always amazed me how much quackery and bad medicine goes on. The temptation of being worshipped and pushing snake oil and making a ton of money at it turns out to be more than most people can withstand.

After being rejected by fourteen publishers, my book *The Eden Express* was published the same year I started medical school. My favorite rejection comment was "This book is good but with your last name it would have to be better."

I took the paperback advance and bought a substantial serious adult-type Victorian house a ten-minute walk from the medical school. When a classmate came over for something, he said that it was the kind of house we weren't supposed to have until we were older.

"I am older," I pointed out. Right before getting the book published and right after getting into medical school, I got married.

The book ended up doing well enough to pay most of my way through medical school—no *Slaughterhouse-Five*, but not bad for a beginner.

Harvard took some flack for admitting me, which probably had something to do with why I shut up and didn't write much for thirty years. There were letters from outraged alumni who knew deserving applicants. With so many earnest wholesome applicants, why was Harvard out dredging for bottom-feeders like me?

My mother, my cousins, and my sisters weren't doing so great. We had eating disorders, co-dependency, outstanding warrants, drug and alcohol problems, dating and employment problems, and other "issues." At least now number one son was married and had a fixed-up Victorian house where everyone could have Thanksgiving and Christmas dinner. What chip on what shoulder? Maybe a man with a compass, a machete, and a strong right arm could lead his people out of the wilderness. If I, as a sick person, had been dragging a dozen or more people down, maybe as a healthy one I could lift up that many or more.

I saw myself as somewhat of a placement problem, and getting into medical school was a huge help. Later, when I was interviewing applicants to HMS and they all had such high aspirations, I wondered if less might not be more. Maybe one of them might say, "I'm just looking for an interesting way to hang out and stay out of trouble." Something like that.

A child ready to learn how to read represents an enormous amount of luck, work, time, and patience. Imagine the astounding luck and work involved in making a medical school applicant. Doctors are like baby oysters on a very deep reef of forefathers and mothers and aunts and uncles hundreds of feet deep with a million important details buried beyond recall. What I asked myself about applicants was whether talking to them made me more or less lonely.

Zachary, my first son, was born when I was two years into medical school. First son had first son so there could be an orderly succession, like the House of Windsor.

✳

Having a famous parent is a leg up to nowhere. It made sense to people that Kurt Vonnegut's son would have mental health problems. It made sense that I would not do well.

"You're Kurt Vonnegut's son? I heard that you had hung yourself in a barn in New Jersey."

"No. Actually I'm in med school."

My mother glossed over the chaos we had come from. "You all turned out so well."

To me it looked like one close call after another and like the woman had been just plain lucky. She could just as easily have a child or two in prison or not getting better from their various disorders and maybe having me hang myself in New Jersey rather than go to medical school.

In general people don't wish the children of famous people well. It's somehow fitting or instructive that we screw up or come to tragic ends. It helped me a lot that I didn't grow up the son of a famous man. It was like watching from afar when the money hit. I'll always remember my father as the world's worst car salesman who couldn't get a job teaching English at Cape Cod Community College.

✳

At Harvard, the courses were pass-fail, but I wanted to get as much right on the tests as possible. I wanted there to be a margin of safety. There were a few of us who would race to see who could finish the tests first. I won more than once. Doing well seemed well within my power.

I loved that *we* had accumulated and organized so much information. I was standing on the shoulders of giants and was possibly the flower of Western civilization. Self-will was running riot, but it was for a really good cause.

Sooner or later in medical school you end up across the table from a senior surgeon with a pair of scissors in your hand. The surgeon ties and holds the suture and says, "Cut."

You cut. He says, "Too long."

You cut the next one a little shorter.

"Too short," he says.

And so forth.

After thirty or forty cuts that are all too long or too short, you ask him if he wants the next one too long or too short, and that's how you pass the test.

I practiced surgical knots until I could do them in the dark. Learning anatomy, microbiology, pathology, pathophysiology, pharmacology, et cetera, was like being on vacation. It was interesting in its own right and I was in love with being able to do it. The questions on the tests had right answers, and because I had read what I was supposed to read and studied what I was supposed to have studied, I knew what they were.

My publisher gave me a copy of Scott Turow's *One L,* an excellent account of his first year at Harvard Law School, but I either wasn't interested in writing anymore just then or couldn't get an angle on medical school that made me want to write about it. If I really loved writing all that much, I wouldn't have gone to medical school. Maybe it wasn't so good for a guy like me to spend too much time alone with a typewriter.

✳

It amazed me how angry some of my teachers and much of the psychiatric profession was that I had been treated with megavitamin therapy. There were two instances in large lectures where I was all but mentioned by name as promoting quackery. I felt like I had been kicked in the chest by a horse and would have thrown up except it would have drawn attention. I was just a guy still in his twenties glad to no longer be in and out of psychosis. I didn't think the vitamins had much to do with my recovery, and I did nothing to promote vitamin therapy. It just happened to be what they were doing at the hospital I was hauled off to.

The megavitamin docs and their critics all seemed like self-absorbed babies whose interest in helping patients was outweighed by the joys of self-righteous vehemence. Their primary interest was in yelling at one another.

A pox on both their houses. Where are the adults when you need them?

Gradually and carefully I'd stopped taking most of the vitamins. It didn't seem to make any difference. So when I discovered my own enlarged thyroid in anatomy class and the doctors at Harvard's Health Services suggested I stop taking the lithium, I didn't think much about it. It was increasingly clear that there wasn't really much wrong with me anyway. I had been started on lithium by one of the "vitamin doctors." He didn't change my diagnosis but said, "You're the kind of schizophrenic who gets better on lithium." This was all pre–*DSM III,* the modern way to slice and dice mental illness. The only thing I really had come to believe in, more than any specific therapy, was the medical model itself, which got rid of shame, blame, and other hurtful voodoo. That was worth doing.

The basic science and the preclinical courses were easy. I was looking forward to learning how to use a stethoscope and those cool little lights and how to draw blood. We practiced on one another and ourselves until we were ready to be unleashed on the world.

After a year and a half of amphitheater/classroom learning, we put on white coats and learned medicine by pretending to be doctors with people who really were patients with the whole show being overseen by people who really were doctors in real hospitals.

If you're not sure what to say to a patient or the patient pauses for a while in his story, what you say is, "That must be hard for you."

✳

I remember staring and watching carefully as our Introduction to Clinical Medicine instructor easily took a patient's hand and gently stroked his arm. I wanted to be able to do that. I was moving from a world where I couldn't touch people I didn't know to one where I could.

It was an advantage for me, over most of my classmates, to know that I was in medical school, at least partly, to save my own life.

We knew some things in amazing detail, right down to the microscopic and molecular level, like how cholera kills people. And over the years cholera has killed a ton of people; there were accounts of cholera epidemics where dehydrated corpses were stacked like cordwood. And now, because we understood it, we could prevent it and/or treat it. All those people who would have died from cholera and been stacked like cordwood got to do something else, like maybe have a son or daughter who went to Harvard Medical School.

✳

There were no stains whatsoever on my coat, which was so white it glowed. I was an HMS II—Harvard Medical student, second year—doing Introduction to Clinical Medicine hoping I might stumble into doing something right or good or at least not humiliate myself too badly.

"Excuse me, but I'm one of the new HMS IIs, and the monitor and the guy next to the nursing station right back there both look really bad."

"Thank you," the nurse said kindly as she walked me back to the room. She looked briefly at the monitor and pulled the door closed.

The patient had had a heart attack at home and his family had gotten the heart going again but hadn't done the breathing part of CPR, so his brain had been deprived of oxygen too long for there to be any hope of recovery. We were just watching him till he died, which was what he was in the process of doing. The nurse told me that the family came in every evening and that this would be a relief to them.

The breathing stopped after a few gasps. The monitor showed a flat line. The nurse unclipped his leads, looked at the clock, and noted on his chart the official time of death. We sat there quietly for a bit. Then we both had lots we had to do. I had gotten to be thirty years old without being in the same room when someone died.

Unless you like being unpopular, never mention that saving a life is a "for now" sort of thing.

✳

Most of the patients I learned from as a medical student and then as an intern and resident would never be admitted to a hospital today because they are *not sick enough*. Because inpatient stays cost insurance companies money and insurers control the vast majority of a hospital's income, the push to get a patient home starts as soon as the patient hits the door. Leukemia, heart attacks, major infections, et cetera, have all become outpatient diseases. If you're not sick enough to be in an ICU, you can probably be treated as an outpatient. As soon as you're out of the ICU, you're discharged to rehab or chronic care. Medical students, interns, and residents don't get to know their patients or see how things turn out; much of what they do any given day is transfer and move people around. It's all about placement.

My first patient in internal medicine was a cheerful seventy-five-year-old Italian. He was admitted for something else, but because he drank a quart of wine a day, I put him on Librium to prevent the DTs like the resident told me to. We turned our only bright spot on the ward into an unresponsive, openmouthed-snoring, bedridden lump. "Well, at least he didn't seize," said the resident.

Being six years older than most of my fellow students had some advantages. After being up all night I looked more like an attending. I was the only one in my class to have a baby at home. During some clinical rotations you were supposed to sleep over at the hospital. Ninety-nine times out of a hundred there wasn't anything for us to do, so I sometimes went home, where I had real responsibilities, to sleep in my own bed and get up with my own fussy baby. I told them to call me if they needed me.

With the exception of one or two people who were there to please their parents, everyone at medical school was there because they wanted to be and had worked hard to get there. We all expected to do important things. We all expected to be part of something like what medicine had accomplished between 1950 and 1975. We expected medical care to transform society. The idea that we would ever be told what we could and couldn't do by insurance companies would have seemed far-fetched and bizarre.

There are a million lives going by at a million miles an hour, and all I could take in was the briefest narrative account of how they came to be in the hospital. There was the passion and energy of a twenty-year-old girl, holding down a job and taking care of her seven-year-old brother who was going to die of a horrible rare cancer; a thirty-two-year-old grandmother whose sixteen-year-old daughter had just had a baby; the father who wanted us to operate on his daughter's inoperable brain-stem tumor and put it in his head instead of hers . . . I didn't have time to give any of these stories anything like the attention they deserved. I wrote orders and discharge plans and tucked people in for the night.

My first clinical rotation was obstetrics. My first patient was in labor, and what she said to me after I introduced myself was "Cut me. Take out the baby."

"You're making good progress," I assured her, and she had a beautiful baby about ten minutes later. This doctoring stuff wasn't so hard.

I watched other doctors like a hawk. I worked very hard at learning how to examine babies and children. I still carry in my brain high-resolution images of how the doctors I admired listened to hearts and felt bellies. I kept accounts of what worked and what didn't, when I was right and when I was wrong. Everybody who loved medicine wanted it to be better than it was, and that meant wanting to be a better doctor than you were.

Even most so-called accidents could be studied like diseases with various risk factors: teen gun violence required a gun, a grudge, alcohol, and impoverished future prospects. Take away the preconditions and the harm stops. Figure out what goes wrong and fix it. Goodness emanated from Harvard and a few other centers of excellence and spread in a centripetal manner, pushing back the darkness. Good doctors went out and displaced not-quite-so-good doctors. Better medicines and surgical procedures displaced older ones. Medical science and care from World War II till the time when I entered medical school was one success following another, a nonstop steady climb. There was no reason to believe it couldn't go on forever.

✳

A surgeon in charge of my surgery rotation said that he knew who I was but that he was going to treat me as if I was normal. I sincerely thanked him and told him I would try to act that way.

✳

Like other things we do to protect patients from our germs, hand washing and wearing gloves and masks, scrubs and surgical gowns were adopted originally to protect doctors and nurses from the diseases of the people they were taking care of.

Scrubs were not made to be worn outside of the OR, where they were always covered by sterile gowns, but as soon as the first absentminded surgeon went out of the OR in scrubs, fashion history was made.

Scrubs have no pleats. Except for the patch pocket over the left breast, suitable for holding three-by-five index cards, they are exactly like cutout clothes for paper dolls. When they started using scrubs in the OR they were white, but blood on white looks too much like what it is and bright white under OR lighting was not restful. Now they are slightly rumpled, gray, blue, green, or, more recently, pink. They started using pink in the OR under the mistaken assumption that doctors wouldn't want to be seen in pink scrubs in the cafeteria or elsewhere. Very shortly after the introduction of "OR only" pink scrubs, pink scrubs were everywhere, including neighborhood basketball courts.

If everyone wore surgical scrubs instead of regular clothing, we could save trillions of dollars. There is no other way to fully clothe a person for less than ten dollars.

Doctors on call or stepping out of the OR are so important they don't have time to put on a shirt and tie. Exhausted, unshaven, and wearing scrubs, I was more credible than with a freshly shaven face, pressed shirt, and tie. There was an intrinsic seriousness to what we were doing that made wearing scrubs okay.

Back in Hollywood Hospital, there were no scrubs. The doctors were very well dressed, and the patients were in pajamas. The doctor in charge of the whole place wore baby-blue alligator shoes, drove a light blue '59 Cadillac convertible, and wore what I was sure was the button to end the world as a tie clip.

✳

I wanted to be a good diagnostician. There was a way of touching people that created trust and gave relief from the day-to-day way people treated one another. I was watching and learning from masters. The doctor's job was to shut up long enough to let the patient be the most important person in the room, because she was. There was an unforced and absolutely real respect for people just because they were people. And we, as doctors, were their servants. For all the things that felt wrong, that felt right.

If you weren't an idealist, why would you go to medical school?

During my core rotation most of our patients were eighty-five or older with overwhelming, intractable problems, which we ignored while looking for things around the edges to adjust. If there was something that we believed in, that helped us keep our spirits up, it was the *salvageable patient.*

When one of my fellow students presented a demented ninety-six-year-old patient who went into heart failure because she ate tuna fish, I couldn't help wondering aloud what exactly the point was. Our junior resident told us that the point was for us to learn physiology from fragile patients so we would be ready and up to the task of saving a salvageable patient when one came along.

Richard was a very polite, fastidious twenty-nine-year-old heroin addict who was nervous about letting anyone except himself draw blood because they might mess up the few good veins he had left. I watched his technique closely. Learning how to draw blood and do other procedures was high on my list of interests. He tapped the needle against the skin and tried to bounce it into the vein. He thought he was better at it than he really was.

Every morning the whole team watched as the resident listened to the heart and lungs of each of our patients. Usually he said nothing because there was nothing to say. One morning while examining Richard he stopped and had each of us listen to a spot he had located on the patient's back.

"Those are rales and rhonchi," he stated flatly. "Richard is coming down with pneumonia."

He had one of us write orders for a chest X-ray and massive doses of IV ampicillin. Four hours later Richard was short of breath, running a 105-degree fever, sick as a dog. The chest X-ray hadn't been done and the antibiotics hadn't been given. The one time we had a physical finding that might have made a difference on the closest thing we had to a salvageable patient, the damn orders were written but never taken off. Our resident was closer to tears than mad. Richard did well. If he had been eighty-five, he probably would have died.

※

My father asked me what I was learning from all this. I told him that needing a doctor was a bad sign.

※

It continues to amaze me how easily doctors can walk away from their mistakes. A patient would be sent to the ICU with horrendous complications and zero prognosis, and the surgeons who botched the case could be toweling off in the locker room and chatting about how to bill for the various procedures involved and the upcoming Pats game.

※

The month before I finished medical school one of my sisters had a psychotic break right after she quit drinking. I went down to New York and was a model of tough-minded efficiency, hiring an ambulance and getting her transferred to a better hospital and better care after it was carefully explained to me why such a thing was not possible. That evening I had two Heinekens, a dozen oysters, a big steak, a double of Jack Daniel's, and called it a day. A job well done. The best proof I had that I didn't have a problem with alcohol was that I drank at least a little every day for many years and didn't have any trouble.

※

By the end of medical school, I could walk through an emergency room or an ICU and feel comfortable and know how to act. I owned a solid Victorian house where my mother and siblings came for holidays. I was the only person in my medical school class graduating with a two-year-old on his lap. Right before the ceremony, my cousin Steve taught Zachary how to say, "Pop's a doctor."

"Half of what we've told you is untrue. Unfortunately we don't know which half, and it will be up to you to figure that out," said the commencement speaker.

It was a clever and wise thing to say, but nowhere near half of what we were taught was true except in a very conditional and relative way. We also lacked the support to make use of what we knew, but besides that. . . .

Later, when I interviewed applicants for Harvard Medical School, they were all bright and earnest and planning to help people. I hurried them through all that because I couldn't tell one from the other.

"Yes, yes, yes . . . but what exactly is being a doctor going to do for you?"

※

I wanted life and being a doctor to be like getting on a bike, pedaling hard, and generating good. By going into medicine—working against suffering, disease, and disability—I was set for life with good thing to do after good thing to do and I would be able to make a living at it. To put myself even more firmly into positive territory, I went into pediatrics. If you were going to change the world, it was a good idea to start with people. And if you were going to change people, it was a good idea to start early.

"Sorry I'm late, dear. I was snatching babies and children from the jaws of death."

I thought that as a pediatrician I would be taken care of and protected, that if people knew I was a pediatrician they wouldn't break into my house or mug me, that I wouldn't have to stop and chat after minor car accidents, that my way would be smoothed. I wanted to be someone no one could take exception to.

When I told a professor at Harvard that I wanted to go into primary care, he said that it would be a waste of a Harvard education. He had done primary care. It was easy. With a Harvard education we could cure generations rather than individuals.

So it wasn't enough that I was in medical school. I was supposed to be lining up to cure generations. And I'd thought I was crazy.

Waiting for something to happen

(Vonnegut family photo)

chapter 8

Man's Greatest Hospital

Chance favors the prepared mind.
—Louis Pasteur

I had applied to twenty medical schools and gotten into one. I would have been overjoyed to go anywhere that had "Medical School" in its name. Four years later I was an insider, asking questions about how much responsibility interns had, whether they were supervised by fellows or senior staff, and what program graduates ended up doing.

Massachusetts General Hospital—MGH—seemed nice. I had done a couple of rotations there and done well. During my interview it was more or less settled that if I ranked it number one, MGH would be where I did my internship and residency. A happy person with decent self-esteem wouldn't bother to have credentials as good as mine.

When I was a resident, patients were taken care of quickly, with compassion and respect. They did not have to wait for hours and hours. Their insurance coverage was something we figured out later. There was a sincere, almost naïve belief in science and settling arguments with science and data. Children with life-threatening infections had lifesaving antibiotics in their system as soon as possible after hitting the door. We were fiercely determined to do the right thing for whatever patients came our way.

The beginning of the end was when we were told we couldn't give out advice on the phone anymore; everyone had to be told to come in and be seen. Someone somewhere thought someone might be wrongly reassured or misinterpret what we said or we might make a mistake that would end up with an injured or dead patient and a lawsuit. We were always incredibly conservative about having anyone with remotely worrisome symptoms come in anyway. There was not a single case of things going badly because of our phone advice or any study about phone advice in general that the powers that be were responding to. It was an administrative answer to an administrative concern. Giving phone advice was good for senior residents' training and helped more than a few children get appropriate care for minor injuries and illnesses.

Having patients come into the emergency room to be seen rather than get advice over the phone seems like a small thing, but it introduced a wedge between doctors and patients. The job was no longer to do what was right for the patient no matter what. It was hard enough to figure out what was really best for the individual and obey the ancient dictum "First, do no harm." Now we had to be in accord with risk management, HMO guidelines, managed care, HIPAA, ICD-9 coding, and on and on. Every bright idea that was supposed to improve medical care has made care worse, usually by increasing costs and restricting access. It was a better world when you could call a senior pediatric resident on the phone to help you through a diaper rash or vomiting or diarrhea. Ninety percent of what gets treated in today's ERs at a cost of billions of dollars, zillions of unnecessary tests, and eons of waiting would go away if people could just talk with a well-trained senior resident. The point is supposed to be getting people appropriate help.

I myself didn't like asking for help. My first night on as an intern in the ER, I faced an unprecedented barrage of twenty-plus patients, many of whom were seriously ill. The junior resident, who was supposed to be helping me, went to the library and fell asleep. The senior resident, who was backing him up, was busy in the pediatric ICU. When I was asked in the morning why I hadn't asked for help, I explained that I'd just assumed, being new, that whatever happened was more or less normal and I didn't want to be a complainer.

When I was a junior resident in the neonatal ICU and a little 800-gram preemie was trying to die by rupturing one lung and then the other and then the first one again and the air from the ruptured part kept filling up the chest and squeezing the good lung tissue and the heart, I put in three chest tubes to drain off the air. The senior who was backing me up mentioned on rounds the next morning that maybe I should have woken him up. If another patient had crashed while I was putting in all those chest tubes, I would have, but it seemed under control at the time.

Attitude is everything. I had more than my share of days where IVs all went in, I got spinal taps on the first pass, and I caught everything before it could hit the ground. It was a blend of will and attitude. When I felt well, things went well. I had a Teflon jacket of positive expectation that got me into and through medical school, internship, and residency. The universe wanted me to succeed.

The stark facts about medical care are that needing a doctor is, in fact, a bad sign, and needing an ICU is a very bad sign. The pediatric intensive care unit (PICU) is a great place to disabuse yourself of notions of fairness. Here, whatever doesn't kill you doesn't make you stronger. It makes you weaker and kills you tomorrow or the next day. Things don't even out.

Christmas Eve '81 it was snowing. I was the senior resident in charge of the PICU. There were maybe one or two patients in the unit who had any chance of surviving, walking, talking, and going to school. Most were on ventilators. One had drowned in a wading pool and was resuscitated but never woke up. They called it a near drowning because his heart and lungs and kidneys survived. One boy was brain-dead from being beaten by his mother's boyfriend, but we couldn't let him go because then the mother's boyfriend could say it was us who had killed him. The sweetest little boy in the world with the nicest parents in the world was getting weaker and weaker and couldn't breathe on his own because of some mitochondrial defect. We knew exactly what was wrong but couldn't do anything about it. A patient with meningococcemia in the isolation room looked like she might do okay. A one-month-old who'd had her heart operated on the day before was not doing well. And so on.

I went out of the unit into the hall on my way to the on-call room to have a cigarette and heard gales of laughter. The families of the patients in the PICU were playing charades, gesticulating, shaking their heads, not talking. Just like anyone else playing charades.

For three years, with one week a year off for vacation, I rode my bike four miles to the hospital and back, even in bad weather, every day, sleeping over when I was on call every other or every third or fourth night, depending on the rotation. I was working a one-hundred-plus-hour workweek, but it didn't seem that bad. Sometimes on call I actually got to sleep a little.

I learned everything I could about taking care of sick children. I was in very good physical shape, as fast as the wind on my ten-speed bike and able to beat most people at squash. I was a good intern and resident. In the beginning of my senior residency I was asked if I would consider being the chief resident. I was honored but too much in debt and not getting any younger. At thirty-four, with a second child on the way, I felt it was time to look for a job.

If the thing you're best at is being a resident, maybe you've peaked too early.

∗

My second son, Eli, was born December 3, 1980, the year of my senior residency, right before the charades game in the PICU family room. I loved my children but often had to stop and think of what a good father would do. I was doing my best imitation of a good parent. I was also doing my best imitation of a good husband.

I had a serious sleeping problem and started taking Xanax for it and feeling much better. I associated not sleeping with going crazy. I didn't want to leave it up in the air whether or not I would sleep at night. Xanax seemed to make me the person I was meant to be and had no side effects. One miracle after another.

It was ten years since I had been seriously crazy. I had done medical school and was finishing up residency. The year 1981 was a much better one than 1971.

I wondered how it had all come to pass, but it always hurt when I pinched myself.

✳

It was early spring when I arrived for my last night as senior in charge of the ER, and there was one "expect note." Sometimes there would be half a dozen or more. I checked the crash cart and the laryngoscope batteries. Whenever I was in the ER and had small bits of time with nothing else to do, I'd scan dermatology texts. Sooner or later I'd run into someone with the disease in the pictures and it would click that I'd seen it somewhere, even if I couldn't remember what it was.

> EXPECT: Prince of the River Nile Smith. One-week-old black male with conjunctivitis. Born at home, did not receive silver nitrate or erythromycin prophylaxis.
>
> Care and Protection order. Child must be admitted and treated for presumed GC conjunctivitis.

Gonococceal (GC) conjunctivitis was the number one cause of blindness before there were laws mandating treatment of all newborns. The closest I'd ever come to seeing a case of GC conjunctivitis was a woman who had a positive GC culture one week prior to delivery. There were lots of ideas about what we should do, and in the end we decided to do them all. The mother and baby each received so many different antibiotics via different routes before and after delivery that whatever germs were there were ripped to shreds worse than Bonnie and Clyde in that machine-gun ambush.

Textbooks show massively swollen, very red, weepy eyes with copious pus.

I got a call from the chief resident at Mass Eye and Ear Infirmary. "We have a seven-day-old baby here with eyes that look fine, but there's a care and protection order on him because the parents wouldn't comply with treatment at Children's Hospital. Our pediatric floor is full, so we're sending him over to you. . . . I don't want to make you nervous, but the father has about a dozen very quiet friends dressed in camouflage fatigues and combat boots. Our security people have already talked to your security people."

I had about fifteen minutes before the Smiths could get over to MGH and register, so I headed down to the basement for my last ten o'clock meal. Whatever hadn't been eaten that day and the day before at the ten o'clock meal was dolled up a little and put back out there one more time. Amazing numbers of calories were consumed by deranged absentminded overstressed hospital personnel. It was free. Whenever anyone said that there was no free lunch, I always thought, "No, but there is the ten o'clock meal."

Malvesti Hedley Smith was about five feet nine, 190 solid pounds; he looked like he was carved out of ironwood. He had jet-black African skin, wore designer jeans and a free-flowing bright African-print shirt, and walked slowly on the balls of his feet like he wouldn't make a sound walking through tin cans in clogs on a tin roof. It was hard to look at Malvesti and not feel inferior. He checked out the waiting room briefly and ushered in his wife, their one-week-old son, and three colleagues in battle fatigues and combat boots. They took stiff seats in hard plastic chairs.

"Prince of the River Nile Smith," called out Helen, the triage nurse, just as she would call out any other name.

Mother with babe in arms, Malvesti, and three friends rose in unison and allowed themselves to be led into one of our small exam rooms.

"Undress the baby down to his diaper so we can take his temperature and the doctor can examine him," said Helen.

"My baby's only problem is with his eyes. He has been examined many times. We prefer that you not take his temperature. I would like to talk to the doctor in charge." Each word was clipped, enunciated perfectly and with a slight British-colonial accent that suggested English wasn't his first language.

His wife, Asanti, was a very pretty, soft-featured, medium-complected young woman of about twenty, one or two inches taller than her husband. The three friends were all about six feet tall, clean-shaven, athletic, in their mid-twenties, distinguished only by their military attire, ramrod-stiff posture, and deference to Malvesti.

Malvesti had a spooky left eye that would break into herky-jerky circles while the right stared fixedly ahead. Then the left would be drawn back into line as if by gravitational force. I tried to map out what pathways must be broken to make his eye act like that but couldn't help finding it just plainly unsettling. He also had ceremonial scars on his face.

"Every patient has to have vital signs taken before being seen by the doctor," explained Helen, who stood a good four inches taller than Malvesti.

"I will see the doctor now. I do not want you touching my child."

"What's going on here?" I interrupted cheerfully. I had been watching and listening through the two-inch round hole in the door. "I'm Dr. Vonnegut, the doctor in charge tonight." Any senior resident in his right mind would have sat back and let the intern handle the case. The truth is that I got bored when I wasn't taking care of patients, and this case seemed way more interesting than most.

"He doesn't want to undress the baby or have us take his signs," said Helen, rolling her eyes behind and over Malvesti.

"It can't hurt to talk a little before taking vital signs." Sometimes I make myself gag.

Helen rolled her eyes again and left.

I reached out my hand to Malvesti, who ignored it. I did my best to ignore that he ignored it. If I was armed with a stun gun and a baseball bat and Malvesti was blindfolded with both hands tied behind his back, he could have destroyed me in a minute or less. I knew from his patient-registration data that he was thirty-four years old, almost exactly my age.

"I am expecting that you will tell me what is necessary to make sure my son does not go blind from the infection in his eyes."

"I promise you that we will not let this infection harm your son's eyes," I said, standing slightly stiffly and speaking with a clipped, vaguely British-colonial accent that made it sound like English was maybe not my first language.

The baby was resting quietly in his mother's arms. His eyes were not even a little bit red or swollen. There was a very small amount of crust where the upper and lower lids came together at the nasal bridge.

"I understand from the last place we took our son that the germ that might blind him is one that is passed by sexual activity. I do not have any symptoms of disease, and my wife has never been with another man. How is it possible for our baby to have this germ?"

At Children's Hospital Malvesti and his wife had balked at allowing the doctors to swab their son's eyes or apply antibiotic ointment, insisting they be allowed to treat him at home.

There were now nine sidekicks in battle fatigues left in the waiting room. And more and more of our beefy security guys milling around.

"The doctor there filled a care and protection order," I said. "If a doctor thinks that parents are not acting in the best interest of their child and that their child might be at risk of serious harm, he can ask a judge to temporarily give custody of the child to the hospital," I explained.

"We will do the ointment and go home now," said Malvesti.

I later learned that there were twenty-four state troopers backing up hospital security out front.

"We believe in preparedness and self-defense but not hurting people. It's very good for the morale and discipline of my men to be taken so seriously," said Malvesti.

Everyone else was blending into the woodwork. "I'm afraid I'm going to have to make some calls," I said.

The judge was not in a good mood. No compromises, no deals: Prince of the River Nile Smith would be admitted for observation and treatment of conjunctivitis that wasn't really there.

"There will be no blood tests or injections, right?" Malvesti asked, realizing that the trap was swinging shut.

"I'm just the doctor in charge down here." My heart was in my throat, and racing. My goal right then was to not throw up.

"You will stay with him of course. And when the culture comes back negative, you can go home and forget about this place. I'm sorry."

Malvesti looked like he had a bad taste in his mouth and nowhere to spit it out.

Half an hour after the family went up to the floor, Louis, the weasel of a junior resident who would be Prince of the River Nile Smith's admitting doctor, called me. "Do you have any idea what was in the herbal compress they were using? There was a case once where a baby almost died from herbal tea."

"The eyes don't look all that bad, do they?"

"No, they don't now, but I'm not comfortable admitting this baby without doing some sort of a work-up."

"We already have done a work-up, Louis. MEEI has the cultures cooking. And we're observing the baby."

"It's my case, and I can't see the harm in doing a septic work-up."

A septic work-up means obtaining blood for culture and complete blood count, urine for culture and analysis, and spinal fluid for cell count and culture. Most unnecessary tests have the good manners to come back normal. But if they come back abnormal, you become obliged to do more tests to confirm or refute the abnormal test. You can end up miles from where you started chasing your tail.

Lynn, a cheerleader-type bubble-brain fourth-year medical student, did the procedures. She got blood on the first stick, the lumbar puncture on the second pass, and the bladder tap. She stopped by to talk with me in the emergency ward.

"What's wrong with the dad's eye? It almost seems like he can control it and uses it to spook people."

"It's central," I said.

"Oh. Thanks," said Lynn. "Louis has agreed to no more tests unless the baby acts sick or has new symptoms. The dad must have taken off while we were doing the tests. At least his mother's still with him. Is it true that black people are better at breast-feeding?"

I tried to sleep on the sticky black vinyl couch in the chief resident's office. In a fitful half-sleep dream I watched myself bent backward across Malvesti's knee, him pulling my head back by the hair with his left hand as he transected my heart with the knife in his right, entering my chest at the anterior axillary line between ribs nine and ten and pulling it to the midline.

A few hours later I got up, had some coffee, and went to senior rounds, where we discussed Prince of the River Nile Smith and all the other admissions from the previous twenty-four hours.

"There was absolutely nothing wrong with that baby," I was compelled to throw in.

"There might have been," countered Louis, "Besides, there was a court order. We had to admit and treat that baby. It was the people at Children's who gave us no choice."

On to the next case. As I got on my bike and pedaled home, I half hoped that Malvesti or one of his lieutenants might run me over before I could cross over to the Charles River.

✳

I had a job lined up with a small respected pediatric practice. In a month I would be calling the shots, doing my best to keep kids out of emergency rooms and getting tests they didn't need.

There were pediatricians practicing in their eighties who still seemed to be having a good time with it.

*

The last thing I did as a senior resident was to transport a critically ill newborn girl who was thought to have an overwhelming infection from an outlying hospital to Mass General. I made the guess, which turned out to be correct, that she had congenital heart disease even though she didn't have a murmur or blueness or any other sign of heart disease. I treated her for heart failure instead of infection and she responded well and survived the trip back to MGH. Her heart was 100 percent fixable. Instead of being dead or crippled, she would grow up with as good a chance as the rest of us.

When the cardiologist praised me to the parents and said that their little girl hadn't been hurt by her rough start and was going to grow up 100 percent normal I felt sick and couldn't get out of that room fast enough.

I was just doing my job. It had been a lucky guess. I hadn't actually diagnosed the specific cardiac defect their daughter had.

*

The day after I finished my residency, my mother had an operation that was supposed to be for a uterine fibroid that turned out to be stage-four ovarian cancer. I hadn't admitted to myself the possibility of something being seriously wrong till I got the phone call.

Enthusiasm

(Vonnegut family photo)

chapter 9

Crack-up Number Four

It's important to me that I owned the house
they took me out of in a straightjacket.

I loved the rhythm and rank of being a primary-care pediatrician. I started paying down the money I had had to borrow to get through medical school and residency. I'd tried to cut down a few times but still smoked two packs of cigarettes a day. I'd take care of a couple of patients, go out to my car to have a cigarette, and come back and see a few more patients.

I was dealing mostly with self-limited viral illnesses in otherwise well babies and children, but life and death wasn't the point. I didn't feel *less than* neurosurgeons, oncologists, or cardiologists. Someone had to be looking through the haystack to find treatable diseases in salvageable patients. Leukemia or brain tumors would always be trying to sneak through, and I was ready to catch them. Maybe I was the catcher in the rye.

I didn't want to be rich or famous. I didn't want to write again. I wanted nothing more than to keep doing pediatrics forever.

For a year or so before I went crazy for the last time, an odd feeling of panic would take hold of me almost every night driving home from work. I'd feel sick to my stomach, my heart would race, and I'd have chest pain. I'd imagine getting into accidents or getting dragged out of my car and beaten. I went to a cardiologist, got on a treadmill, and passed my stress test. He reassured me that my heart was fine and joked that it was nice seeing me but that he had to go take care of sick people.

He asked me about alcohol and drugs, and I told him I drank a few beers after work, had half a bottle or less of wine with dinner, maybe a shot of bourbon after dinner, and Xanax as prescribed for insomnia. He said nothing, so it must have been okay. Apparently what I had used to be called "soldier's heart" because so many soldiers complained of the same thing during World War I. I was a good soldier. Crushing chest pain and nausea were just part of being me.

My wife and I were two cordial, barely connected children of divorce who mostly wanted no drama. The harder I tried to be a good husband, the worse it seemed to get. She was married to a doctor—what more could she want?

My sisters and I were on good terms. I was glad they were married to decent men and having children. We all knew Jane had cancer that wasn't going to go away, but she was doing remarkably well.

Man Recovers from Mental Illness, Goes to Medical School, and Becomes a Doctor. It was a perfectly good story with a perfectly good ending.

✳

For about ten years running, Kurt had hosted a family fishing trip out of Montauk, near his place on Long Island. It was usually the weekend after Labor Day. It was usually an all-guy thing, though sometimes my father enjoyed inviting Betty Friedan along. We were all fighting our own battles, looking for some time off, and willing to show up for Kurt and see what happened. Bluefish are, pound for pound, the most vicious of God's creatures, and we caught a lot of them.

Bernie, Kurt's older and only brother, usually came with two or three of his five sons and sometimes a grandchild. Sometimes my sons came with me, but not on the 1985 trip. Kurt and Bernie would tell the same stories and jokes. I knew most of the punch lines, as did Bernie's sons.

Bernie was Kurt's only real peer at that point in his life. Eight years Kurt's senior, he was a scientist who did things that hadn't been done before, like seeding clouds to make it rain. My favorite experiment of his was the release of several tons of chicken feathers into thunderclouds to see where the air currents were going. Kurt and Bernie's sister, Allie, the mother of the four cousins who came to live with us, had been a gifted painter and sculptor who said, "Just because you're talented doesn't mean you have to do something about it."

One of my favorite stories about Bernie and Kurt involved a trip they took to see their father, Kurt senior, when he was dying. On the way to Indianapolis, the car they were driving ran out of gas, so they were going to hitchhike to a gas station. Kurt propped the hood up to let people know there was mechanical trouble and asked Bernie if there was anything else they should do.

"We could let the air out of the tires," suggested Bernie.

On the 1985 fishing trip, Bernie brought twenty glass-and-gel plates he had used to record the path electricity took through gel under different conditions. The branching patterns were intricate and beautiful. Bernie's provocative question to Kurt was whether or not they were art. Kurt thought they weren't art, because the objects weren't made by an artist who could have a conversation with himself or anyone else about what he had done. For it to be art there had to be an artist who could learn from it and do something different or the same the next time.

Maybe Bernie, by noticing these things and dragging them to Long Island for us to see, was the artist? You can't create or destroy matter or energy, but you can take blank paper and write a novel or canvas and make a painting or wood and make furniture. An artist is someone who isn't put off by how terrible his first tries are, who finds himself talking back and notices that he changes and grows when he makes art.

That trip was the beginning of the end of what I had assumed was a lifetime no-cut contract with alcohol. I can't remember why, but I drank much more than I usually did, and nothing happened. I drank beer steadily through the morning and then had two glasses of bourbon. No click, no feeling a little looser, nothing.

We caught a bunch of bluefish. The mate filleted them and I grilled them over charcoal with garlic salt and everyone said they tasted great just like always, but I couldn't get away from the feeling that another shoe was going to drop.

What if you pick up the early signs too late?

Back home, I was playing the piano better than ever. I'd be playing the piano and singing and start crying after a beer or two. Unless we had a business lunch on Friday, I never drank at work or before getting home, somewhere around 6 P.M. I sometimes kept beer in the office refrigerator on Fridays if I was going to be going to the Cape, but that was okay because of the traffic. If I had had a drinking problem, I would have hidden it, but I didn't so I didn't.

The thing that keeps the gambler gambling is the illusion that he has control, special knowledge that will make him come out on top. If the gambler comes to believe that he is up against a random number generator and that what he once thought of as special knowledge is worthless, he stops gambling. What keeps the drinker drinking is the certainty that she can stop whenever she wants. It never would have occurred to me that stopping the pathetic little bit of drinking I did would have mattered.

I kept in touch with MGH by serving as the ward attending once a year and teaching in the ER one night a week along with admitting my patients there. It was a way of giving back. They paid me about sixteen dollars an hour.

Four years after I'd finished my residency at MGH, right after Thanksgiving, a twelve-year-old girl came in having had a seizure that had stopped by the time she arrived. We examined her, drew labs, reassured her parents, called her pediatrician, and had the resident doing pediatric neurology come down to see her. He started her on medication, decided she didn't have to be admitted, and set up a time to see her in the pedi-neuro clinic two days later.

Off the top of my head I gave the medical students a ten-minute lecture on the differential diagnosis, work-up, and treatment of pediatric seizures. I was a hardworking, integral part of a wonderful hospital and a wonderful medical school and a wonderful city, full of people all doing the best they could. I was headed off into the sunset with two hours of movie left.

My final drink was the stale last half of a two-dollar bottle of red wine I'd hoped might taste more like a ten-dollar bottle, guzzled and gulped through chopped cork fragments left behind by a paring knife when the corkscrew failed to get the job done. I had rules that guaranteed I would never get into trouble with drinking. If I broke a rule, I had to stop drinking for a week to prove there was no problem. Finding myself drinking the bottle I had recorked after dinner violated both the half-bottle-of-wine-per-night rule and the no-alcohol-after-Xanax rule as well as the not-being-pathetic-and-desperate rule. All the trouble that followed that night could have been avoided if I had just taken an extra milligram of Xanax and stayed in bed where I belonged or if I hadn't had so many stupid rules.

When I stopped drinking the next day, I threw in the Xanax as a generous gesture. The first twelve hours went well. "If you do something every day, you won't be able to figure out what it's doing to you unless you stop doing it," I kept repeating. I was an almost-forty-year-old, home-owning, married father of two boys who was on the faculty of Harvard Medical School and who coached soccer.

Time started stretching in unpredictable ways. Maybe orange juice would help. My first appointment that morning after slugging down a quart of orange juice was a mother who wanted to talk to me about her son's alcoholism. Once your moorings come a little loose, that sort of thing happens and happens and happens until you just can't pick yourself up off the floor anymore. Snowflakes hit with the force of Mack trucks. The floor and ground got a little springy, sort of like I was walking on a trampoline.

The next morning I was trying to get dressed, and I woke up in a puddle of spit not able to move. Maybe if I just drank more orange juice or gin, I could pull things together and my wife wouldn't notice anything.

I read the chapter in Goodman and Gilman, the basic pharmacology text, about alcohol withdrawal and was amazed. Suddenly, alcohol went from being 0 percent of my problem and possibly the glue that was keeping me together to 100 percent of my problem. There was no evolution. But now that I knew what the problem was, everything was going to be okay.

"Oh my God, you're a pig."

I had dressed up a pig and put lipstick on a pig and thoroughly fooled myself and then taken a pig out dancing. Chilled mugs, imported beer, no more than six or seven a night, Bordeaux futures, never more than half a bottle of wine most nights, making a quart of Jack Daniel's last a month—all lipstick on a pig. Drinking less than I did in college, blacking out at most once or twice a year . . . more lipstick on a pig. Having one or two reasons your drinking is okay is maybe okay. I heard someone at a meeting say that on her list of all the things that might be wrong with her life, drinking too much was number nineteen.

All that fancy wine in my basement was nothing but alcohol. What was I going to do about the couple thousand dollars' worth of Bordeaux futures I owned? I cried tears of joy for having been such an idiot and having things now be so clear. It was also an enormous relief that, since I knew what the problem was, I wouldn't have to do anything degrading like go to a hospital.

I went to an ATM and took out two hundred dollars. A man not sure of where he's going or what might happen next needs at least two hundred dollars. I called my sister. She was seven years sober at the time, and I asked if she could take me to an AA meeting. We went to a meeting at the Kennedy skating rink in Hyannis. Amazingly, I won the raffle and was given a Big Book.

"It is a *big* book," I remarked to my sister. "And blue. Do my hands look like they're glowing to you?"

When I put a twenty-dollar bill in the collection my sister said I should have only put in a dollar. I said that if these guys were going to save my life, I should give them at least a twenty. I liked the meeting a lot. There was no mention of Bordeaux futures, but I did notice that people were trying to tell the truth and the point was to save their own lives.

✳

At meetings I've heard people say proudly that they have no original thoughts, that everything they say they learned in meetings or from reading the Big Book. Wouldn't that be nice? I have so many original thoughts I have to take medication for it.

✳

Somewhere in there my psychiatrist made a house call. He was very comforting and reassuring. I told him that I was very afraid and didn't know if I could make it through the night. He said everything was going to be okay and left me with a roll of one-milligram Ativan pills and told me to take one if I got nervous. I think there were forty pills in the roll. I called him again in the morning and told him I was nervous again. He seemed surprised when I told him that all the little white pills were gone, and he thought maybe I shouldn't go to work.

"Maybe I should go to another one of those meetings?"

I went in and out of being okay and would try to reassure everyone. *Don't worry, I get it now. I'm really going to be all right.* But people were less and less reassured.

I was utterly cooked. I prayed a very simple prayer: *"God help me."*

And something answered: *"Okay."*

Which I took as divine reassurance that things would work themselves out. I didn't take my cousin Jim's suggestion that maybe I should go to a hospital all that seriously. I had God's word that everything was going to be just fine. Maybe I'd go to a hospital once I had things figured out a little better—I didn't want to confuse people. I didn't want to be overdramatizing my situation and taking up a space in a hospital that might be needed by someone who really had a problem.

Miracles are no one's fault, I'd think, and I'd be unable to stop laughing.

✳

When the voices came back it was like they'd never gone. Fourteen and a half years, and it was like we picked up in the middle of a conversation that had been interrupted just a few minutes earlier.

Having music and art speak to you and move you to your core is a beautiful, beautiful thing, but whenever it happens I can't help worrying that the voices and too much meaning are lurking around this bend or the next or the next.

"Testing testing testing. Mark, can you hear me? Mark, come in. Can you hear me?"

"Yes, I can hear you."

"Thank God, we were afraid we had lost you. Don't worry, everything is going to be okay now."

"Could you please get someone else? I've served my time and am much too old for this crap. Can't you let me be sort of normal for a while? Fifteen years ago I did a hell of a job standing up for righteousness, but it damn near killed me and took me a long time to get over. I just think you could find someone else."

"You're the best, Mark."

I always assume that if I'm hearing voices, everyone is hearing voices. It's not hearing voices that's the problem. The problems come when you try to do something about the voices or mention them to others.

What made the police wrap me up in a straightjacket and sheet and take me to the hospital was an utterly sincere, full-force attempt to dive through a closed third-floor window. Without a moment to waste doubting, I had to run as hard as I could and do my very best to jump through the glass, or I would know forever that I had failed and at least one of my sons would die. I tried to jump through the closed window to prove that I was capable of faith and worth saving and not just a selfish little shit. Luckily most of the glass and sash went out and down into the bushes and I bounced back into the room.

God Himself had told me everything was going to be all right. My version of "all right" did not include chatting with the voices and being chucked back into a psych hospital. I was so quickly in tatters, what was the good of all that overachievement? It should have taken longer for my proud crust of wellness to be so utterly gone.

I had no argument with the police wrapping me up in a straightjacket and taking me to the hospital. I had tried to jump through a window and was acting in an erratic manner. But they didn't have to be so rough. I'm not very big and have never hurt anyone, and I had only tried to jump through the window to prove to God I was worth saving. I tried to explain: As soon as I proved my faith, all the bad stuff was supposed to stop. The voices and agitation and need to do things to stop worse things from happening was supposed to go away. It didn't.

The most arrogant outrageous thought is that there's a point in thinking.

There was a little sand in my gearbox.

A small thing wrong can make a big thing go completely wrong.

It wouldn't make sense for God to set up a universe where He had to keep track of every sparrow and step in and fix things with miracles. Better to have billions of sparrows and check in less often.

*

Part of what happens when one goes crazy is that there's a grammatical shift. Thoughts come into the mind as firmly established truth. There is no simile or metaphor. There's no tense but the present. The fantastic presents itself as fact.

It would possibly be tolerable to feel *like* or *as if* one was on fire or *like* the CIA might be after you or *like* you had to hold your breath so that you could be compacted and smuggled to a neutral site in Mongolia to wrestle India's craziest crazy. But there's no *like* or *as if.* It's all really happening, and there's no time to argue or have second thoughts.

Without prelude or explanation, I'm in four-point restraints in my boxer shorts on a gurney in a side hall of the hospital where I once trained and currently still work. I'm HMS alum, HMS faculty—I actually teach Introduction to Clinical Medicine and the Newborn Exam—and I didn't even get into McLean's?

"Don't worry about me," I explain to strangers passing by. "The police way overreacted. As soon as my doctor gets here they'll undo these silly restraints. Do you know that in a well-run hospital, restraints are almost never necessary?"

Without being too self-centered and petty, I couldn't help wishing that they had either let me get some clothes or not taken me to the hospital where I was on staff, or if they had to take me there, why couldn't they have put me in a quiet little room somewhere, anywhere but the hall, please?

A nurse whose kids I had taken care of for years passed by looking afraid and like she might cry. "Don't worry," I tried to tell her. "This will turn out okay."

It's probably possible to gain humility by means other than repeated humiliation, but repeated humiliation works very well. Fourteen years earlier, I'd fought my way back from being crazy with a lousy prognosis to write a book and go to medical school, finish an internship and residency. Now I was married with two kids, locked up in a windowless room, again. I was being treated with Haldol instead of Thorazine and weighed about 180 instead of 130. Long run, short slide.

✳

In a totally unscientific survey of RNs done right around the time of my fourth psychotic break, I was named the number one pediatrician by *Boston* magazine. Truth is stranger than fiction.

*

I had prayed and God said things would be okay and I assumed it meant okay without my having another breakdown or having to go to the hospital. God was a lot less wordy than the voices. He also neglected to say anything about my marriage, which was unlikely to be improved by my hospitalization and not being able to work for a while.

I had a memory of throwing rocks that I had grabbed from an aquarium at my wife right before I tried to go through the window. That wasn't like me. We had seen two marriage counselors at that point, and I should have had at least a clue that things might not work out no matter how little she or I wanted to get divorced.

*

During my first break, the content of my delusions involved questions of human existence that went back to the beginning of time. This time it seemed largely about the advantages of free-market economies. Nuclear war would be averted and the Berlin Wall would come down if I emerged victorious. Anyway that's what I was told. It boiled down to me against the Russian Bear. *The hopes and fears of all the world are met in thee tonight.*

Win or lose, the cover story would be the same: I was crazy of course, in a hospital of course. The department will deny all knowledge of your mission.

"I'm here to stop the war," I explained. "I don't really care that much about free-market economies." It seemed like I was getting dragged into disputes of less and less caliber. Free markets? Next they'd be summoning me to settle zoning disputes.

The voice of God is in the wind.

There's nothing in the world to be afraid of. There's nothing that's not in the world.

You are in the palm of God.

"Does that mean I don't have to wear seat belts? What about saving for college or retirement? Could it all be just silly?"

Beguiled again, a child again, bewitched, bothered, and bewildered.

I was on a quiz show again.

"John Coltrane was from South Carolina. High Point, I believe."

Why aren't there more questions about early Christianity?

It wasn't so much the voices, but I wished everyone wasn't dying and going away forever. I wished I didn't have the feeling there was something I was supposed to do about everything. I wished we could go back to not having everything be so important. There's always an earthquake somewhere.

Someone could no longer remind me of someone without actually becoming that someone. The difference between hearing something that sounded like my name and hearing my name was the difference between sleeping in my own bed and waking up in that windowless room where big people come and give me shots.

Put on all the armor of the Lord. Not just the pretty stuff.

Why is there so much meaning when the mind breaks? Why isn't it just static or nonsense? I became convinced that my being willing to wrestle the Russian Bear could avoid a nuclear exchange and save millions upon millions of lives, not to mention the planet, from nuclear winter. The content of the voices and visions constitutes a hazardous nuisance to someone like me who so likes to figure out puzzles.

The first time I went crazy I thought that good things might come out of it. I looked forward to learning whatever it was the voices knew and how they knew it. I thought it might be possible to acquire powers that could be used for good. I was asked to save human existence and wanted to do my part.

In the seclusion room I was riding a pendulum that would swing from the past through the present into the future and back again, though that wasn't all there was to it. There would be times, very brief times, when I was okay and could understand and make myself understood and where it wasn't all lurching gobbledygook. Before I swung out of the present and was really nowhere again, I wanted to wake people up and tell them I was okay so that they wouldn't give up on me.

I was a late entry in a very complicated battle of the beatitudes, in lieu of war, where the poor the hungry the sick the naked the meek of all cultures and nations could settle arguments and avoid bloodshed. I didn't argue as much as maybe I should have, but my capacity for faith and supposition and quick connections was a lot of why the job had fallen to me in the first place. I had handlers who packed me in cotton and foam and smuggled me across borders. It was important that I be very still and quiet and keep my eyes closed.

What do you have in there?

There were passwords.

"You don't want to know."

Where's the princess?

"Okey-dokey."

The eagle has landed.

The bear doesn't want to talk about it.

"You want me to do *what*?"

They would put me next to someone else from somewhere else, and I, or they, would win. It had something to do with depth of human feeling. It was like we were in a stadium full of utterly quiet, meek, sick, poor, hungry people who decided to back either me or the other quiet, packed-in-cotton-and-foam person.

"So the meek really do inherit the earth," I thought.

When I won, I went forward to the next round with the backing of all the people who had backed the person I had beaten. The losers went back to doing whatever they had done before after having their memory erased. Nothing bad happened to them.

I kept winning round after round. Having my memory erased and going back to whatever normal was would have been more than fine with me. All of China gave up without even trying.

"We have some crazy people here, but no one that crazy." And it was on to the next round.

During this time the hospital billed Blue Cross Blue Shield for two thousand dollars' worth of psychotherapy I don't remember.

The thread that was to help me succeed in getting to wrestle and prevail over the Russian Bear was the joke about the courageous Indian brave:

There's a young warrior who is told by the shaman that he can have a long, happy life and save his father from the loan shark, his tribe from starvation, whatever, if he . . .

1. Climbs an unclimbable mountain and brings back the tail feathers of an eagle from the nests on top of the unclimbable cliffs.

2. Wrestles a polar bear.

3. Makes love to a beautiful princess.

He climbs the mountain, scales the cliff, gets the tail feathers, then comes back to the village, his clothes and self bloody, torn, and tattered.

"So where is the princess I'm supposed to wrestle?"

Yip di mina di boom di za

What's the white stuff in bird poop?

"That's bird poop too."

Explanations of what was going on and why were presented by the voices. *You know that you are dead. You know the world is ending. You know it's up to you. Package it up. Put a skim coat on it and hope people think it's a wall.*

There were five teenagers in the dayroom who threw things at me and called me *doctor.* I was an injured lion circled by Rhodesian ridgebacks. I hoped one of them would slip and get close enough for me to grab.

There are no grown-ups.

There will be no reckoning.

The day before the day before Christmas 1985, in the dayroom where the five mean teenagers ruled, I went up to the very overweight curly-haired girl I knew was the Russian Bear and said, "Do you want to dance or what?" and she fled crying. It was pretty much the end of Soviet-style communism. They took me back to my room like nothing big had happened.

It was over. I tried to explain my theory of grammar and psychosis to the people at the hospital, and they listened politely.

✻

If

If you come to weighing ten pounds less than you remember yourself weighing . . .

If there are a bunch of psych patients hanging around outside a door you can't open or lock . . .

If big people come through the door, angry, like maybe you gave them a hard time the last time they came to give you shots without so much as a hello how's it going or goodbye . . .

If you think about what it was you were thinking just before all hell broke loose and you get a little nervous . . .

If you find yourself thinking it *again even if you can't remember exactly what* it *is . . .*

Then you are a nut, my son.

✻

My hospitalization was all black and gruesome punctuated by daily moments of peace and light when they gave me pathetic little fragments of Xanax around 5 P.M. For twenty minutes or so there would be hope in the world and color and then it would fade and I'd wait for 5 P.M. the next day. Never trust a drug that's spelled the same backward and forward and has two x's in its name.

I was not addicted to Xanax. That would have made me a drug addict. I just needed it to breathe. Six years of drinking a little every day with a little Xanax to help me sleep = no trouble. One week of no drinking, no Xanax = big trouble. It's not easy to go from being one of the seven righteous pillars holding up the planet to being just another mental patient.

My frightened eight-year-old son came out of the fog to visit me in the hospital. I wished very much that he didn't see me like that. Maybe having kids was pushing things too far.

Big strong man, strong right arm, machete, will of steel, had managed to hack his way deep into the jungle.

"Things will get better, Zachary." I vowed I would fight through hell itself (might as well, since I was already there) to make this moment go away and not be what my precious son remembered of his father. My mother looked at pictures from her childhood and saw a mother not able to look at or pay attention to her little girl. She was not sure for how long or how many times her mother was hospitalized.

✳

At any given point there are several million people in this country who are psychotic. As a matter of law they are exempt from being judged responsible for their actions while crazy. They are also 99 percent invisible. Most won't get better enough to be as well as they were before. Many won't really get better at all, just another part of life to not look at if you don't want to get depressed. I've read studies indicating that 90+ percent of the homeless are mentally ill.

Things do not even out.

Jane at age fifty-five

(Photo by Michael Cullen)

chapter 10

Coming Home

Drinking a little every day, I had come to live in a small
space where my feelings were very big and scary.

It was the day before Christmas, 1985. I was thirty-eight and
seven-twelfths years old. I wanted to come home from the hospital under my own steam. I took a taxi most of the way and
walked the last half mile. The third-floor window I had tried to
jump through had been repaired, but there was still glass and
broken sash in the bushes. I had three Christmas ornaments I
had made in art therapy in my pocket. I have them still; regard-
less of how "good" the music or painting is, the arts have been
a lifeline and the heart of the matter for me and Kurt and many
other people.

When I was getting ready to leave the hospital I would look
at my hands like they were someone else's. It was the damnedest
thing how they shook and trembled. I had always had a mild in-
tention tremor, but I prided myself on doing medical procedures
well. I needed at least an approximate sense of where my finger-
tips were and what they were up to.

The first time I managed to speak up and ask a question at an AA meeting, I asked, "How long does the shaking last?"

"You drank a long time, you're going to shake a long time," said a gravel-voiced woman named Hope.

While I was still in the hospital I had to sign something about my disability insurance. "Too bad it doesn't really insure against disability," I thought. My father sincerely said it was a good thing I had disability insurance, and I wanted to yell at him. How would anybody be able to tell if a writer and an icon was disabled?

Before, I'd been seeing twenty or thirty patients a day. I thought it was keeping me sane and at the same time proving to the world that I was cured and making me a living. I thought things were fixed and okay forever. Right before all hell broke loose on the commune, I had thought that things were all right and fixed forever.

※

Jane defied the odds long enough to see several more grandchildren born. When asked, I regretfully told her that stage-four ovarian cancer wasn't a curable disease. She said that none of us knew the future and that something else might kill her, like getting hit by a truck. When I was in the hospital wrestling the Russian Bear and standing up for free markets, my mother's cancer came back and no one knew how to tell me.

She was in the hospital being operated on again when they told her that I was in the hospital. I had just finished opening Christmas presents when they told me her cancer was back.

I cried. It was a bad December for the home team. We didn't deserve to be having things going so badly. Would it have been that hard to stagger my mental illness and my mother's cancer by a couple of months?

I looked out from a home that I somehow owned. There were two cars in the driveway. I had been to medical school and done an internship and residency. For the moment, anyway, I had a valid license to practice medicine in the Commonwealth of Massachusetts. Work wasn't eager to have me back like tomorrow or the next day, but no one was saying I was done forever. I was related to the person who had done all the hard work that made the house, cars, et cetera, possible, but it was a complicated relationship. I couldn't imagine what it would be like to see patients again but guessed that maybe I could do it if that was what I was supposed to do.

Maybe I just had to learn to be comfortable with being uncomfortable, with being scared out of my mind, and to let it go past like it wasn't about me.

✳

The place I felt most welcome and comfortable was AA meetings, even though there was a sticky-sweet optimism there I found insufferable.

"The grace of God won't take you where the grace of God can't keep you."

"You never get more than you can handle."

"You won't die from not drinking or not sleeping or being afraid."

"Ha."

The people who had died from not drinking or sheer fright were respectfully dead and quiet and unavailable for comment. I was quite sure I was going to be one of them. I had slowly and carefully consumed a lethal dose of alcohol and alcohol equivalents and would eventually die from either drinking or not drinking. My biggest problem was figuring out how to get word back to these cheerful pabulum peddlers when I died from not drinking. I wanted to have a gravestone carved: "Mark got more than he could handle."

> Happy Joyous and Free, the fine print.
> It's only fair to inform you that if you manage to not drink,
> your capacity to suffer and endure is going to be increased
> by several orders of magnitude and you are going to need it.

✳

Had I been any sicker for very much longer back in the seventies, I wouldn't have recovered enough to think about going to medical school and no medical school would have let me in. I had put together a good chunk of well time—fourteen years— but now there was a substantial chance that if I didn't get my act together reasonably quickly, I'd be put out on the curb with the rest of the trash.

One month after the hospital, I was depressed and had the zip of a soggy potato chip, so someone ordered an EEG or brain-wave test. It was mostly normal but showed *generalized frontal slowing.* It didn't seem to worry my doctors much, but it seemed ominous to me. Maybe the threads on my screw were too worn down for me to be able to practice medicine again. I wasn't arguing. I just wanted to know if generalized slowing was something people got better from or not.

I missed alcohol very much. Those little slivers of Xanax they gave me in the hospital had made me feel so very much better, it made sense that if I could just have one or even half a beer, I would be able to sparkle just a little and maybe complete a thought and be a better father or be able to read a newspaper. I wanted to be the guy who everyone thought should be a pediatrician again.

My partners took me to grand rounds at MGH, where I thought everyone was looking at me. I appreciated the change of pace and their time but wanted to blurt out, "When can I come back?" knowing it was exactly the wrong thing to say.

My wife said I wasn't the person she had married and she couldn't stand having me hanging around the house. I'd spent my whole life believing that by force of will I could do things and make things happen. I just wanted to be a normal guy who was married and went to work and had kids, but it all seemed to be slipping away.

My second son, Eli, was sick a lot. I had brought home respiratory syncytial virus from the hospital when he was a few months old. RSV for most people is just a bad cold, but with babies it can go down into the lungs and, as it did with Eli, set them up to become asthmatic. He was five years old when I came home.

Eli never complained but spent a fair amount of his early childhood sitting on the couch coughing and wheezing. He would get pneumonia two or three times a year, during which he'd throw up everything and run 104-degree fevers. He didn't grow much. It didn't help that until he was four his father still smoked.

When I stopped drinking, Eli stopped getting sick. He fattened up a little, grew a sneaker size, and started playing sports. Six months into my experiment of living life without the buffers of drugs and alcohol, it all became too much. My father was impossible, my mother was dying, I had a horrible fight with one of my sisters, my wife didn't like me even a little, there wasn't enough money. I begged my psychiatrist for some Ativan. I didn't even like Ativan. I certainly couldn't get addicted to a drug I had so little affection for. Half a milligram later, I felt instantly better and it became clear that Jack Daniel's had never been anything but a good and true friend. Within a day Eli threw up everything and spiked a fever to 104 with what proved to be his last pneumonia. He's now taller than me, which I don't mind, and I've been drug- and alcohol-free ever since. About all I was good for during the first months of recovery was wrestling and hanging out with Eli. That had to be enough, and it was.

✳

Somewhere in there I started painting after ten years off, at first with oils and then back to watercolors. I did it in the basement so as to not wreck anything. I bought a Yamaha digital piano and started working on jazz standards. I started writing a novel about a depressed pediatric senior resident who gets run over by the angry father of a baby who gets mistreated in the ER. When I wanted to take music-theory courses at the New England Conservatory, my wife became exasperated; surely there was something I could be doing to get back to work faster. Why wasn't I taking a medical course of some sort?

"You're a doctor," she said.

Was I a drug addict or an alcoholic or just plain crazy? There were all those questions on the medical license renewal application to deal with. The chief of pediatrics at MGH knew I had been hospitalized. He liked me, so I more or less followed his lead when he described the problem as a drug problem that I had gotten into by taking drugs as prescribed for my sleeping problem. To me it seemed a little bit more complicated than that, but if I was going to have a shot at continuing to practice medicine, I had to give people a simple, easy package to swallow.

Because I hadn't screwed up medically or acted out in a professional setting, I didn't have to report to the Board of Registration of Medicine. In AA meetings I was an alcoholic who also used drugs, but mostly as prescribed. Purists said that if you were a drug addict who also drank, you were supposed to go to different meetings.

An earnest, bright-eyed young man at an AA meeting told me that to stay sober most people couldn't keep doing whatever it was they had been doing for a living before they got sober but that perhaps I could work in a bookstore until I figured it out. I had to face the possibility that I could lose my profession, but it seemed like a terrible waste of all those premed courses and then medical school and then internship and residency. What was I going to do to pay the bills when the disability insurance ran out?

Two months after being hospitalized, I met with my partners and my psychiatrist to try to figure out when, if ever, it was going to be okay for me to come back to work. It was a tentative, very soft-spoken, slow-moving tea party. I tried to be dull without being too dull. Everyone was doing the best they could.

I was on lithium, which had been restarted during my hospitalization. Lithium is a mood stabilizer, yet my mood seemed anything but stable. I wanted to be stable and could have been stable by using the mood stabilizer that came in cases of twenty-four returnable bottles and tasted really good in chilled mugs or the more concentrated stuff in the bottle with *Jack Daniel's* written on it. I could have been a lot more like Clint Eastwood and less like me and probably more popular.

It would have been almost logical to ditch the notion that alcohol was part of my problem. Alcohol had, in fact, been mostly a comfort that had brought me safely through many bad times. Ninety-nine times out of a hundred I felt at least a little better with every drink. Except for maybe the seizure when I stopped, alcohol and I had gotten along very well, and maybe the real issue was Xanax.

With four psychotic breaks to my credit and a solid four-straight-generation family history of hyper-religiosity, voices, delusions, et cetera, I more than met diagnostic criteria for bipolar disease, formerly known as manic depression, which was why I was taking lithium. Why did I want to crud things up by bringing alcohol into the picture? If you're an alcoholic, you don't have to take lithium. You just don't drink. If you're bipolar and take your lithium, you can probably drink a little. It seemed unlikely, over the top, gilding the lily, and almost bragging to say that I could be an alcoholic and a drug addict and bipolar. Where's Ockham's razor* when you need it?

But there was something about the intensity of the vision that alcohol was not my friend. I would have rather eaten putrid flesh off the bone than had another drink. Just because I could drink and be okay with it didn't mean I had to drink.

The next Christmas I took a big bite of coffee cake that was loaded with bourbon and spit it out against the wall.

"Walnuts," I said to the startled bystanders. "I can't stand walnuts."

At a certain blessed point you are able to just not drink without thinking about it all the time.

---

*Ockham's razor is useful when choosing between two theories that have the same predictions and the available data cannot distinguish between them. The razor directs us to go with the simplest of the theories. William of Ockham in the fourteenth century: *"Pluralitas non est ponenda sine neccesitate,"* which translates as "Entities should not be multiplied unnecessarily."

I wasn't sleeping. There were times when I went several days with no sleep at all.

My mother was slowly relentlessly crushed from the inside and eaten up by her cancer. Together we wrecked two Christmases in a row.

"*Uncle, uncle, uncle,* damn it. Didn't anyone hear me call *uncle*?"

I was acutely aware of a gritty stiffness twisted into every muscle of my body, as if I was on a spit being roasted over a slow fire. It came and went without there being anything I could do about it. I was painfully aware that I couldn't drink, which is what anyone in his right mind would have done. God bless the moments when I felt all right.

After I'd been hanging out at home for a few months, a doctor who admired *The Eden Express* and ran a small psych hospital in Florida offered to pay an honorarium and for my whole family to fly down to Disney World if I would come talk to their staff and patients. I enjoyed being a professional and trying to give them their money's worth. I didn't tell them I had been crazy again and was just a few months out of the hospital.

I ate steamed blue crabs off of newspaper-covered picnic tables and liked that a lot. Maybe this was what Tigger does best.

Shortly after that, my partners let me come back part-time and then full-time. It was a huge relief to be doing something I knew how to do and could get paid for. Maybe in some sense I was and still am addicted to taking care of other people's problems. Faced with sick children and worried parents again, I felt useful.

✳

There was nothing to do for my mother except to be with her as much as possible while she was dying. When she looked around the Cape house, which she had treated more like a friend and co-conspirator, she was radiant and proud and whole. She had come from very little and created a great deal for many, many people. At the end, she toned down the "Aunt Jane" and acknowledged what my sisters and I had been through. She talked without rancor about Kurt and she said she was glad I didn't drink anymore. Her initial response had been "Oh no, you're not an alcoholic. You're a nice boy."

※

During the Bow Wow Boogie that year, three months clean and sober, in the ninth inning of the final game, I threw out a runner trying to go to third on a dribbler out in front of home to preserve the tie. Then I drove in the winning run with a single in the bottom of the ninth. It was no more or less likely than the Red Sox that same year going on their incredible run to get into the World Series and then blowing it with the soft grounder that went through Buckner's legs. Baseball was something to count on in this crazy world.

With mental illness the trick is to not take your feelings so seriously; you're zooming in and zooming away from things that go from being too important to being not important at all. So I was watching my thoughts in a detached way. I could zoom in or out to see how they looked without trying to change them. If I was lucky, I might find things that could be part of how I try to tell the truth.

The first truth is that none of the thoughts going by are worth drinking over.

✳

Alcoholism and mental illness aren't very different and I had both. When I believed that I was well because I worked hard and made good choices... when I believed I was well because I deserved it... I was living in a shoe box. My worries were my enemies, and my best tool was my ability to hold my breath. I was, in fact, a good doctor, and that seemed important, but the importance kept pleading for itself in a way it shouldn't have had to do.

Amazingly, during or shortly after that last break, something broke through the thick plate-glass barrier between myself and the rest of the world. I didn't have to stop and think anymore about what a good father or a good friend or good husband would do.

✳

At the end of my drinking I had a baby-poop-brown underpowered Subaru that I picked out in the dark when my underpowered baby-poop-brown VW died. The three cars I've had since have been a sleek black Honda Prelude with four-wheel drive, a red pickup truck, and a red Mini Cooper S with racing stripes and the extra thirty-seven horsepower.

Sometimes when we're stopped at lights, other drivers look at me, and I look back at them like "Who are you looking at?" before I realize it's my car.

✳

When I could hear music again I noticed Coltrane, Monk, Professor Longhair, Billy Strayhorn, Stevie Ray Vaughan, Aaron Copland, and some others like I had never heard them before. They too seemed to be trying to tell the truth to save their own lives, and I was intensely grateful.

Pelotas

(Photo by Mark Vonnegut)

chapter 11

Honduras

The real root of all evil is how hard it is to do good.

Two and a half years after my last psychotic break, my wife and I were on our fourth marriage counselor. I had moved most of my clothes to the basement and slept there. We didn't talk about it. She said things were fine.

An emergency-room doc friend named Max mentioned that he was going on a medical/dental mission to Honduras. I asked if I could come along. I'd have to chip in eight hundred dollars for my travel expenses and go to three or four organizational meetings on the Cape.

Max was a tall, handsome extrovert whom I had known from MGH, but we became friends when we met again in AA meetings when I was first trying to get sober.

I know you, he seemed to yell as he lunged across the room. He was much too big and much too loud. I had kind of hoped that an anonymous program meant that nobody knew anybody.

He asked me how I was doing, and I said I knew I was doing great because I had a ton of alcohol in the house and wasn't even a little tempted to drink it. Max came home with me and poured my half bottles of this and half bottles of that down the sink so that if I slipped, it would have to be on vanilla extract or mouthwash or rubbing alcohol like everyone else. Thanks, Max.

✳

At the organizational meetings, we were told over and over that the people of Honduras would be very grateful. Most of them would have never seen a doctor before. We would not be dealing with worried well people. There would be lots of previously undiagnosed disease and chances to make dramatic saves. Back home the patients were so thoroughly picked over there were more chances to mess up than to do good. Helping people was easier if they hadn't already been seen by a million doctors. There would be no forms to fill out and no malpractice worries. We had more than three thousand slightly used tennis balls to hand out, donated by tennis clubs on the Cape.

Dentists could line people up and pull their rotten teeth and make them better without a single word being exchanged. Plastic-surgery teams could come down to Honduras and fix cleft lips by the dozen without necessarily getting to know their patients or even having to speak Spanish. Optometrists were going to do vision exams and match up people with discarded donated glasses. Pediatrics doesn't involve a lot of one-hit good deeds, like repairing a cleft lip or pulling an abscessed tooth. It wasn't clear to me that much of what I could do lent itself to people lining up with their kids for one-time encounters. I'm a better doctor when I'm seeing fewer patients an hour and when

I speak the same language they do and when I'm going to see them again. But we did have all those tennis balls to hand out.

Treating sickness as a business opportunity has just about killed the joy of healing, the very reason most doctors and nurses wanted to go into it in the first place. Part of what was so attractive about the Honduran trip was that none of us would be making a dime on it; our care was to be free to the patients. We would be tending to the sick because they were sick and for no other reason. The problem with trying to comply with quality-improvement initiatives and worrying about lawsuits and coding guidelines and all the other stuff we have to do is that doing the right thing for the patient gets buried in all the muck. It's like trying to be an Olympic high jumper with ankle weights. The Honduras trip would be free of all that other stuff. There would be nothing for us to do but the right thing.

At our last organizational meeting, just before we left, it was announced that we would be staying in a coastal resort, Hotel Villas Telamar, rather than being put up by native Hondurans and sleeping in hammocks. The first two trips had been strictly dental, with less than half as many people involved. Because this was a much bigger expedition, finding enough natives to put us all up in hammocks had turned into a logistical nightmare. Villas Telamar was an all-inclusive beach resort, formerly owned by United Fruit and used as a resort and housing for its executives and their families. They gave us a really good deal. I still wasn't the world's greatest sleeper and was frankly relieved by the prospect of a bed in a hotel instead of a hammock in a hut.

We had two hundred volunteers: nurses, doctors, dentists, optometrists, pharmacists, translators, and all-purpose helpers. There were more than a hundred crates of donated supplies and medicines. We were each paying most of our own travel expenses, with local fund-raising and charities covering the rest. A couple of drug companies were chipping in. We were all giving ten days of our time to help the poorest people of one of the poorest nations in the hemisphere.

✳

Short time here, long time gone. The reason to try to be good, smart, kind, and on the side of angels is because it's more fun and because there really aren't any angels.

✳

It took us eighteen hours, on three flights and a long bus ride, to get to where we were going: Tela, Honduras. Gavin Archibald, a dentist from Texas who had recently married his office manager, was in charge of the mission. On the longest leg of the flight, from Houston to San Pedro Sula, I fell asleep and dreamed I was back in junior high. I had no clothes on. Everyone else was dressed. I had a baseball glove. No one else had a baseball glove. It wouldn't be fair to have figuring out dreams be important to mental health.

There was a physical therapist named Crystal who might have been flirting with me. She gave me a neck rub during the layover in Chicago, and I would have followed her anywhere. Even with my marriage going poorly I hadn't dared to even so much as flirt with anyone else prior to this.

By coincidence the prime minister of Honduras was with us on the flight from Houston to San Pedro Sula. He and the dentists from Texas were chatting, sipping drinks, in the front of the cabin like they had gone to Andover together. The prime minister made an impromptu speech to us about how important and significant and needed our mission was and how grateful he was and how grateful the people we helped would be. He mentioned that the Haitians manipulated the data when they claimed to be the poorest country in the hemisphere and that it was in fact Honduras that had the lowest per-capita income and highest infant mortality.

At the welcome banquet, dessert was a flan loaded with rum. Max, who'd been sober ten years, was wolfing down the flan till I grabbed his spoon, interrupting the rapid round trips to his mouth.

"*Rum,* Max."

"What?"

"The flan is full of *rum.*"

"Oh."

✳

The resort had swimming pools and a pure white sandy beach with a main building and numerous outlying bungalows. Each bungalow had a refrigerator with distilled water. Before I was fully awake, I brushed my teeth with tap water. We'd been told not to do that.

"Remember to brush your teeth with the bagged water," I told Max.

"Of course," said Max.

Max insisted that I turn over all my cash and identification to him. He would keep it safe in a brown khaki bandolier money belt under his fresh blue paper scrubs. I would get to wear the money belt the second half of the week. I had forgotten how much fun it was to have a roommate.

"I'll keep a little pocket money," I said.

"Sure," said Max. "Just ask me if you need more."

I walked the beach early in the morning and found a dead dog, legs up, bouncing in the surf. It could have happened anywhere.

On the way to breakfast I saw very well nourished vultures in the trees and nicely dressed laughing kids atop two-hundred-dollar dirt bikes.

Breakfast was fruit and eggs and bacon with waffles from overflowing platters on a giant buffet table or omelets cooked to order. The Reverend Calvin Peters, an Argentinean who made a living shepherding medical missions like ours, got us each to give him a few hundred dollars, which he would exchange for us for Honduran lempiras so we could have some spending money. He said that he could get us the best deal, since he would be exchanging a large amount. He also posted sign-up sheets for shopping trips he would arrange so we could buy local arts and crafts.

Peters was a smooth, soft man with thin arms and legs, silky silver brushed hair, and a small round belly that made him look a little bit pregnant or like a python who had swallowed a baby pig. His wife, who joined our trip with him in Houston, was about twenty-five years old and Barbie-doll bouncy.

We spent most of Sunday setting up the clinic so we could see patients the next morning. The clinic was going to be in a school. A peeling faded wooden sign announced ESCUELA J F KENNEDY. I got a lump in my throat.

Next to the school were weeds that looked like twelve-foot-high asparagus stalks, bearing individual red and yellow fruits the size of candlepin bowling balls. Subfreezing temperatures and the changing seasons give New England foliage a certain seriousness and discipline. I've never looked at an oak or maple tree and thought that there might have been a different way to do things. Here, next to the bright colors of the plants, the school's gray concrete and gray wood trim made it nearly invisible.

Mark Twain said, "Coconut palms look like feather dusters that have been hit by lightning." I wished I'd said it first.

The school had no plumbing or electricity. There were no windows, just chain-link mesh where windows should have been. For blackboards each room had a square section in the middle of the front wall where the concrete was more smoothed out than the rest of the wall. There was a one-story building and a two-story building, neither very big.

The dentists took the one-story building because it had a porch; they set up three dental chairs and could work in the open with plenty of air and sunlight. There were five dentists and five dental assistants who manned the three chairs in rotation, twisting, pulling, rocking, chiseling, and leveraging rotten teeth. People waiting to see the optometrists and doctors watched people get their teeth pulled while they stood in line.

Kids in the courtyard made impressive human pyramids and played soccer with a crumpled paper-and-tape ball. By the end of day one, they would all have tennis balls.

The optometrists took the upper floor of the two-story building, which normally was the school principal's office. That left the bottom of the bigger building for the medical team. The adult doctors wanted to see some kids. I didn't want to see adults.

There was a chiropractor with an adjustment table who liked kids and others looking on while he cracked necks and spines.

I had an Ambu breathing bag with a full set of pediatric masks. I shoved two desks together to make an exam table. I had solutions to clean wounds, antibiotic ointments, sterile gauze and triangular bandages for slings, IV catheters and solutions, a stash of IV antibiotics, and five hundred 3x5-inch index cards. I was going to make out a card for every patient I saw. If I had managed to keep up with the index-card idea, five hundred wouldn't have been enough.

An internist who had been on an earlier trip said that virtually all the children would be malnourished and infested with parasites and that we should worm them all, but the kids playing in the school yard looked healthy and well nourished.

It was late Sunday afternoon by the time we had things set up and ready to go. Patients would start lining up at seven the next morning, and we would start seeing them at about eight. We boarded our sweltering hot chartered bus and waited to be driven back to the resort.

Tela and the surrounding towns were plastered with posters announcing the clinic. A charter bus company was planning to run buses from La Ceiba, sixty miles east. What we didn't know, because none of us had seen the posters, was that every patient was expected to make a contribution of one lempira, about forty cents, for each doctor they saw.

That night we had a meeting in the same room where three weeks earlier the presidents of several Central American countries had worked out a peace plan that was unacceptable to the United States. You had to go up ten steps to reach the podium, reminding me of the Whaleman's Chapel in New Bedford from *Moby-Dick*.

The first speaker was Lorenzo James, a midsized dentist from Texas dressed in battle fatigues with surgical tubing, Kelly and straight clamps, and several sizes of needle holders hanging from his double-punched black leather and steel eyelet belt.

"How does that surgical equipment stay sterile out in the field?" I asked Max.

"Without him this trip wouldn't be possible," said Max. "He's the president and founder of the Foundation for Medical and Dental Care for Central America." President George H. W. Bush had declared Lorenzo James a Point of Light.

Along with the clinic at Escuela John F. Kennedy there would be a mobile unit that went out into the bush, as they called it, with two Land Rovers. They would set up in remote village squares and take care of whoever needed taking care of, sleeping in the homes of villagers and moving on when they ran out of patients.

Among the positive attributes of the Honduran people cited by Lorenzo James was their deep gratitude for the help we were bringing, their hospitality, and the fact that they bled less and required less pain medication than patients in the United States. The germs in Honduras were less likely to be antibiotic-resistant, so small doses of penicillin usually did the trick. The children were very brave and rarely cried. James told a joke about malpractice insurance.

The next speaker was Dr. Sandor Martinez, the chief of service and only surgeon at the local hospital and commissioner of public health for Tela and the surrounding area. It was under his auspices that we would be practicing. He would arrange follow-up care for anything we thought needed follow-up. He mentioned that the local doctors and dentists weren't thrilled with our presence. It had never occurred to me that there were local doctors.

"The Hondurans are a very conservative and dignified people. Please don't wear shorts except in the resort compound. Please don't pull any more than four teeth from any one patient. You don't know what happens when you leave. Some of these patients bleed and bleed and we can't transfuse them."

Three teachers from the school, one of whom was pretty, said through translators how grateful they and the whole community were that we were there. They knew they were closing the school for a week for a greater good.

The last speaker was the school principal. He was a maybe five-foot-tall Mayan who smiled only briefly and spoke perfect English. After the bare minimum of pleasantry he said that what the school needed more than anything else was a new fence and that they would be setting up a gate to charge patients one lempira per consultation. The teachers would man the gate.

All hell broke loose.

"We're like a bake sale," I said to Max.

Could we make a cash contribution or come back later and put up a fence ourselves? It was important that the care we gave be free, that people not have to pay.

The principal shook his head. If we were here to do what was good for them, we could start by listening to what it was that they wanted done, and what they wanted was to charge one lempira per consultation and use the money to buy a fence.

It became clear from the discussion that Calvin Peters had known all along about the fee and that he himself had been paid a fee by the school to recruit our mission. When we got the money he had gathered from us at breakfast it was three days later and at an exchange rate considerably less favorable than that offered by waiters, cabdrivers, and assorted street urchins. Exchanging dollars for lempiras made no sense anyway, as there was not a merchant in Honduras who wouldn't gladly deal in dollars. The rev was doing nicely for himself.

Lorenzo James was outraged and urged a boycott of the clinic we had spent all day setting up. We should just run shuttles with the Land Rover and go out into remote villages like he and his crew were planning to do and as the previous two missions had done.

"They're a very proud, grateful people. They have no money but bring food and carvings. No one in the bush has ever seen a doctor. Forget the clinic."

The pharmacy, the optometry equipment, and lots of the other equipment we had set up wasn't very portable, and who was to say the school principal and teachers and community would want to let us come and go as we pleased if we weren't taking care of patients?

"Could we wear shorts in the bush?" I asked Max.

We offered the school two thousand dollars cash to let us take care of people for free. No go.

Max said that if we had to charge, maybe we should make it more like five dollars a head and see if we could come away with some real money. No one laughed.

So if we didn't open and run the clinic as advertised, what would we do? Visit Mayan ruins and fish for the twenty-pound largemouth bass I had heard existed in a remote lake? Maybe just chill at the beach resort? I would have been more than a little disappointed to have come all that way, set up my little area, and then not be able to see how it worked. We should have offered them ten thousand dollars and found ways to take most of it back like third-party insurers do.

A little after midnight, Gavin Archibald, our fearless leader, got up and said that we couldn't and wouldn't shortchange the Honduran people. We would have one of our translators at the desk monitoring the teachers collecting the money, making sure no one was turned away. We were professionals and certainly weren't going to refuse to treat thousands of people over a lousy forty cents per patient seen.

At breakfast it was announced that anyone who wanted to could be taught how to pull teeth and that the four-teeth-per-patient limit was silly. There is a fancy word for twisting and rocking back and forth while you pull that sounds like the fancy word for burping.

A hospital in Rhode Island had donated two thousand sets of blue disposable paper scrubs, enough for each of us to have a fresh set every day. A battalion of white people in dazzlingly bright blue scrubs descended from the blue-and-white bus and took their places in the school clinic, watched by Hondurans who had paid their fee and were waiting patiently. There were adolescents on bikes with assault rifles strapped on their backs in lieu of police.

On the first day of our clinic the nurse practitioners and I saw 187 patients. Nearly 100 more were given vouchers assuring them of a good place in line for the next day. There was as little or less wrong with most of the patients I was seeing than was usual back home. Most of them were well-nourished, bright, healthy children who didn't eat what their mothers thought they should or who coughed, usually without fever or waking up or any other symptom. Two children in the first hour were for second opinions on hernias. In both cases Sandor Martinez was right: the umbilical hernia would get better by itself; the inguinal hernia would not.

Once people pay, even if it's only forty cents, the expectations and entitlement follow as night follows day. The people controlling the gate had no incentive to not ram as many people as they could through the one-week-only-see-the-Yankee-doctors moneymaker.

I had three twelve-year-old girls from the local Catholic school translating. They sometimes did it by committee and would argue among themselves about what it was that the patient or I was trying to say. "Bones ache," "Baby no eat," and "Cough" were the most common chief complaints.

The first "Baby no eat" I saw was a beefy thirty-pound two-year-old with wrist rolls, chipmunk cheeks, and a Buddha belly. "Baby eats," I said. "Maybe the neighbors are feeding the baby or the baby gets up and raids the refrigerator when the mother is sleeping." The translators looked back and forth nervously.

Of the babies and children complaining of cough, almost none of them coughed. I never figured out what "Bones ache" meant, but I weighed and measured everyone and asked about whether or not they ate or coughed and if the bones ached more during the day or at night and showed them where their child was on the growth chart, and everyone seemed happy.

One of my first patients was brought up to the front of the line by our triage nurses right after he had a grand mal seizure. He was back to himself by the time I saw him. He was a strong, handsome, nonverbal boy who had had six to eight seizures a day for many years. His mother was a small, shy, pretty woman who looked like a teenager herself. It wasn't the seizures she was worried about but the fact that for months he had been holding his penis and screaming while smashing the wall with his other hand whenever he had to pee. She couldn't look at me for more than a millisecond. It was just as well that I didn't speak Spanish so we didn't have to say *penis* back and forth.

There was no discharge; the penis looked fine. It could have been a bladder infection. I had brought a couple hundred urine dipsticks from my office that could tell me in minutes if there was blood or protein or sugar or white cells in the urine.

"Just a small amount of urine in the cup," I explained to my translators, who passed it on.

He seemed to understand what he was supposed to do and put a small amount of urine in the cup and a much larger amount in a giant arc on my cardboard partition while he screamed and punched the wall.

His urinary stream was excellent. The urine in the cup was normal. I had brought the full weight of medical science to bear on his simple problem and had come up empty. I didn't have the faintest idea why he held his penis and screamed when he peed.

I tried to explain that he could have a lot fewer seizures a day with medication and wrote out a note to Sandor Martinez. The boy's mother was politely trying to seem interested. I gave one of our tennis balls to her son, who nodded appreciatively and rubbed his cheek with it.

The boy with the seizures and over half the other children I saw had scars on their shoulders from smallpox vaccinations. I'm sure there's been no smallpox in Honduras for many, many years. If you're a pharmaceutical company, nothing goes to waste.

His mother asked if she had to go back outside and get into line and pay her lempira all over again to be seen herself. I took her across the building to introduce her directly to Max with my translators. Max was under the impression that he spoke Spanish and started doing so at the small, shy woman, who shrugged and looked hurt and confused. Max is big and energetic in any language.

"Speak English, Max. Use the translators. Your Spanish scares people."

Our baby-blue paper scrubs didn't hold up well in the heat and humidity. By noon they were falling apart. Bellies and underwear were flashing. Someone was dispatched to go back to the compound to get more. Cloth shorts would have had advantages. Our money belt was plainly visible wrapped around Max's glistening belly.

"Be careful, Max. I think they can see our valuables."

While I was over on the adult side, someone asked me if I'd help hold down a twelve-year-old boy while they were draining an abscess, so I grabbed a leg and helped out, wondering if the kids with something wrong with them were ending up being seen on the adult side and I was the "baby no eat–bones ache– cough" specialist. They got about five cubic centimeters of pus out of a not-very-swollen lymph node. Wouldn't antibiotics and hot compresses be just as likely to work? What did we know about abscesses in the tropics and the risks of making a surgical incision in someone you might or might not see again? What if we slipped and nicked a big vessel or nerve? We put a draining wick in, gave his mother a prescription for Keflex, and told them in Spanish to come back at the end of the week. What if we had run across this kid on the last day of the clinic? Would we still have gone after that node?

In my regular job, many of the children I see for ear-infection follow-up couldn't possibly have had ear infections. The eardrum has no thickening, no redness, no fluid. There's nothing but a thin, translucent, perfectly normal eardrum. The antibiotics these children were put on couldn't possibly have worked so quickly. Doctors and patients and parents are so eager for the resolution a diagnosis of ear infection brings that phantoms appear and are welcomed. The doctor finds something wrong, thus doing his job. The parents' decision to seek medical attention is validated. The visit is over. Everyone gets to move on.

Now, in Honduras, where I was expecting a stream of severely ill children, I'm suddenly in the same position as the ER doctors back home. I'll never see these people again. A few hours into the first day I see a bulging, bright red eardrum and feel warm all over. The little girl probably had ear infections before and had gotten over them on her own. She would have ear infections again and get over them without a doctor or antibiotics, but I was a happy guy.

"Ear infection," I said to my translator, who passed it on like a great gift to the parent who had brought the child and stood in line for hours.

"Amoxicillin," I said generously as I wrote out the prescription for the parent to take to the pharmacy.

"Should be better in forty-eight hours," I added expansively.

I now know and suspected then that antibiotics have very little effect on ear infections, but it takes longer to explain that than to give out prescriptions.

After seeing another two hundred or so patients on day two, I was a dishrag, dazed and barely able to walk. I wedged myself into a window seat on the bus and waited for it to take me back to the compound. I had promised myself that I was going to swim at least a little every day. There were three doughnut-ring formations of coral twenty yards from the beach. Each ring was about thirty feet across and contained its own little world. There were lots of bright-colored fish riding the swells in and out of the giant doughnuts. There was also a menacing barracuda about seven inches long. I just wanted to fit in and tried sliding in and out of the coral doughnuts with the fish. My legs got cut up pretty badly.

When Max asked what had happened and I tried to explain about being playful, he said it was lucky I didn't attract any playful sharks.

Every day the lines got longer. The charter buses from La Cieba east along the coast started to arrive. Ten of me couldn't have put much of a dent in those lines.

After four days of breathlessly trying to keep up, I met Freddy Ruiz, a small, quiet man who picked his way carefully through the chaos and asked if I was Mark and if I took care of children. I said I was, and he asked if I would come to his orphanage.

My team was more than happy to get rid of me. After three days of martyrdom to a nonstop onslaught I was probably painful to have around. It didn't matter what or how much any of us did. In many ways the nurse practitioners would do fine and maybe a little better than me.

Almost everyone else on the mission had already taken tours of this or that or a beach day or been shopping for native crafts.

There was something very likable and reassuring about Freddy, but my attitude after being held hostage and made to practice pediatrics in a concrete coop for three days was not good. Why didn't this guy Freddy just pile his kids into a truck and have them wait in the forty-cent one-lempira line like everyone else?

Freddy's orphanage was only about thirty minutes away, but I felt better and better with every mile put between me and Escuela JFK. Halfway there it became clear that Freddy thought I was a dentist.

"No, Freddy, I fix just about everything except teeth."

I was invited to see the orphanage anyway: twelve houses with about five to six children and a set of foster parents in each sprinkled over about ten acres of citrus groves. The biggest building was a school with paper and books and art all over the place. There was a giant vegetable garden and a barn with cows and goats and a chicken coop.

It was owned by the Catholic Church, but Freddy was quick to point out, "You don't have to have Catholicism to be a child here."

Since Freddy had taken over, the children at the orphanage were no longer available for adoption. They had only been able to place two or three of the younger children a year anyway, and the rest of the kids and staff just sat around feeling like unwanted failures. Now all the kids went to high school and beyond. They all had jobs and tutors. The comparison with the kids I was seeing back at our clinic, where less than 10 percent were going on to high school, was stark. One thing a Honduran child might consider to get ahead would be to lose his parents and find a way to get into Freddy's orphanage.

A hasty clinic session was arranged. I was ushered into a clean, nicely set up exam room with an office, where, one at a time, children with charts and coherent problems and histories appeared with a bilingual nurse who knew what medications were available.

There were two girls with complex congenital heart disease who had never been seen by a cardiologist. Neither was doing well. Both had a chance of being helped if we could get them to Boston or Miami for catheterization. It turned out that wasn't out of the question and that a note from me would help. I taught them how to make a paste out of aspirin to get rid of warts. I saw about ten kids and started scheming with Freddy and his nurse about getting the useful leftover equipment and medications from the mission to end up in their health center rather than somewhere else.

I stayed in touch with Freddy for several years afterward. One of the girls with congenital heart disease did well after an operation in Miami. The other had had too much blood going through her lungs for too long and would have a shortened life.

By the time I got back to the hellhole I had helped to create at Escuela JFK it was late in the day. John, one of the translators, was in my room with a stethoscope around his neck, putting it on one well-looking child after another.

"All these kids with coughs who don't look sick, which is most of them, I listen to their chest and then give them 250 milligrams of amoxicillin, which is what the nurse practitioners told me to do. We had to do something. They seem happy with it, especially since they don't have to stand in the pharmacy line."

"If you turn the stethoscope around, the earpieces and your ear canals will line up better and you'll hear more," I said.

More than a few patients were taking whatever medication they got from us and selling it to brokers on the street.

When we told people we couldn't see any more patients, mothers pressed their babies and children toward us against the chain-link fence.

"No *pelota.*" We'd run out of the tennis balls after day two.

Friday was mostly spent cleaning up. Two of the doctors from the adult side brought over a beaming twelve-year-old boy whom I didn't recognize until they showed me the wound and wick from where we had drained the abscess Monday. We took out the gauze wick and covered the wound with antibiotic ointment and a sterile dressing.

"We did him some good," said one of the docs. The mother was effusively grateful. I couldn't help thinking how easily it could have been otherwise.

About midnight the night before we left, Max and I borrowed a car and went back out to the clinic site. In the moonlight we could see that nothing was left. A battalion of recyclers must have descended and stripped the place bare. All the cardboard, the wiring, even the litter was all gone. It was like we had never been there. Come Monday they would have school and most of the kids would have new, slightly used tennis balls.

There was a three-hour layover in Houston. Crystal and I got a cab and went shopping at a nearby mall to buy sunglasses and gifts. It was more or less like any other shopping mall. We got coffee and doughnuts and bought Houston Rockets T-shirts, all of which were available at the airport, then made a mad headlong dash to make it back in time for our flight. The flirtation never came close to being anything more, but it scared the hell out of me how much fun it was palling around with a girl.

The pictures I took in Honduras came out well, and I made up a slide show to go along with a talk I presented at senior rounds. The chief asked if I'd consider giving the talk at grand rounds, which was held in the same amphitheater where I occasionally went to AA meetings on Fridays. Out of the blue the dean of admissions of Harvard Medical School showed up in my office, took me out for lunch, and asked if I'd consider serving on the admissions committee.

"Yes, yes," I said. "Yes."

Mark goes mainstream.

If you know how things are
going to turn out, why bother?

(Photo by Barb Vonnegut)

chapter 12

Not Right for *Here*

Normal people do not make particularly good doctors.
They're too good at taking care of themselves to be
able to take good care of strangers.

The Harvard Medical School admissions committee sees a steady line of bright, creative young people who are eager, ready, willing, and able to give of themselves for a chance to be useful. Six thousand apply, eight hundred are invited to be interviewed, and two hundred of those are accepted.

Once the first forty-two hundred or so have been eliminated, the quality of those left is so high that a perfectly good class could be selected by flipping coins and throwing darts. Many applicants rejected by Harvard go elsewhere and become excellent doctors. Except for one psychopath, there was no one I interviewed who couldn't have become a good doctor. Beyond the pool of applicants selected for interviews, there are many qualified people who want to be doctors who can't get into any American medical school and who have to go to Guadalajara or the Caribbean to pursue their dream.

I seriously doubt that my application would have made the first cut against today's applicant pool. No candidate whose application I reviewed or heard of had anywhere near as low an undergraduate math-and-science grade-point average as mine. It's possible the committee members of the day, back then, were distracted by the question of whether or not I was schizophrenic and overlooked my grades.

Interviewees invariably talked about how much they wanted to contribute to society, help people, push medical science forward. When I asked them what being a doctor was going to do for them, often they looked at me like was a trick question.

We rate applicants on a scale of 1 to 10, but you quickly learn that a 9.0 is the kiss of death. I mentioned this to one of my fellow committee members, who said, "Yes, and 9.5 is no kiss at all." If you didn't have all or mostly 10s, you probably weren't going to get in.

The process whereby one gets to be a doctor is one where you pretty much have to be a grade-and-approval junky. This eventually has unfortunate consequences—all a hospital or insurer or pharmaceutical company has to do to get doctors to jump through hoops is set up a grading system and put some doctors in tier one and others in tier two or three or four. The courage to do the right thing in the face of disapproval is often lacking.

There is a dangerous point in the deliberation process of the admissions committee where the application has been formally presented and one of the people who interviewed the candidate briefly defends why he gave the candidate a 9.5 or 10.0. There's a pause where anyone on the committee can say anything. If the next thing that's said is strongly positive, the application will sail on to the next level, but if someone says, "A bit thin on the extras," or "Were they involved in the community?" or, worst of all, "It's a strong application, but is this applicant really right for *here*?" the fate of the otherwise strong applicant twists in the wind. Trying to defend someone at this point almost seems to make it worse. If the application needs your help, how good could it be?

People don't apply to Harvard Medical School lightly. They are all standing on a lot of shoulders. We were passing judgment on some of the most absurdly intelligent, accomplished, highly motivated men and women the world had ever produced.

The curse of having to be important dooms a lot of us. Living up to all that white marble and the tree Hippocrates taught under and the admissions process is not easy. If you become a doctor to make a difference, it turns out that no difference you can make is enough. Unambitious people aren't going to be applying to or getting into medical school, but once an ambitious person gets in, she has to either win a Nobel Prize or learn how to be of service to ordinary people with unglamorous problems.

If it wasn't for questions like "How high's the fever?" "How many days has he been sick?" or "Diarrhea?" I wouldn't know what to say to people. Whether or not children eat vegetables has consumed a significant part of my professional life. Nobody I've interviewed for medical school has said they want to get really good at treating diaper rashes and quieting crying babies and frightened children. Life-or-death comes up less often than you might imagine and when it does the doctor's power to change the outcome is limited. If you're saving your energy for the big important moments, you're going to be saving a lot of energy. People who are trying to die are trying to tell us something.

"What problems are young people having today?" I was asked at a harmless social get-together at the home of the dean of admissions.

The problem for young people today *is* the Harvard Medical School admissions committee. People this bright and accomplished shouldn't have to be begging for a job in medicine. It shouldn't be so hard. There should be more clearly defined, simple paths for people to be of use. That so many young people want to be doctors speaks well for the families producing intact applicants and for medicine for attracting them, but I can't help feeling that there should be a broader array of choices. People that intelligent who have worked that hard should be able to be doctors if they want to. What exactly is the point of producing an abundance of amazingly capable people if we don't have more things for them to do? Two hundred years ago being able to read and write a little, being healthy and having a work ethic, meant you could do well at just about anything.

It shouldn't be so hard for people to figure out what to do with their lives.

"What the hell are we going to do with Timmy?"

"I don't know. Do you think we could get him into med school?"

Every Nobel laureate was once a goofy sixteen- or twenty-two-year-old whose family worried about what the hell he or she was going to end up doing.

I have had heartbreakingly accomplished patients kill themselves or become heroin addicts. It's not enough to play an instrument perfectly or to get a full scholarship.

As soon as a new hurdle is set on the path to getting into

medical school (organic chemistry, higher and higher GPAs, higher and higher board scores, extracurriculars, community service, moving personal stories, et cetera), the ability to clear that hurdle spreads through the applicant pool like the ability to resist penicillin spreads through a petri dish. Everybody is throwing a lot of pasta up against the wall hoping that it will stick. Any essay that works will be reworked and reworked and reworked some more.

Some applicants were accused of trophy collecting. It wasn't enough to be a concert pianist, work in a first-rate research lab, or save a small South American village. It had to come from the heart.

After watching so many candidates I liked go up in flames I suggested to the dean that each committee member be allowed to advance one applicant a year to the final pool without the usual debate. He thought it was a good idea and would bring it up to the committee.

Is a doctor really that special a thing to be, or are we making too big a deal of this? It's like we're all scrambling to get to a place a little higher up on some slippery pyramid because we don't know how high the water will be when the tide comes back in.

✳

Sometimes my father would call me out of the blue. "Is this the doctor on call?"

"Yes, it is, Dad."

"Sorry about your profession. I wouldn't be a doctor for anything. That's got to be the worst job in the world."

✳

When I became a pediatrician, a short visit cost ten dollars, a checkup was twenty. People paid cash. Our overhead was 27 percent. Our books were kept on a yellow pad. We were free to determine the content of the visit, which mostly consisted of asking patients or parents what we could do for them and taking it from there. When medical insurance came into pediatrics, it seemed like a good deal because we would suddenly be paid twice as much for visits and procedures and our patients wouldn't be paying anything out of pocket, since it would all come out of the insurance that was taken out of their paychecks. We also realized we had no choice, since no matter how much they loved us, most families would take their kids where the care was covered by their insurance. We also had to get computers and hire people to track whether or not we got paid and do a bunch of other stuff. There goes the overhead.

In the fine print it became illegal for us to charge the uninsured or anyone else less than we charged our insured patients and it also stipulated that the insurer would pay us at a discounted rate for our charges. The net effect was that my professional services went from something my patients could easily afford to something that, without insurance, they couldn't.

When I ask pharmaceutical salespeople what a new drug costs, they hasten to reassure me that it's covered by insurance and will only cost the patient a ten- or twenty-dollar co-pay. Co-pays are the tip of the iceberg. Without insurance all these new, absurdly expensive medications could not exist. With insurance it becomes suddenly worthwhile for pharmaceutical companies to spend millions and billions pushing less-than-necessary medications to providers and patients. These costs push up the cost of other medications and insurance and care in general. If you believe that the dollars made by the pharmaceutical industry are plowed back into research that leads to better and better medications, you probably believe in the tooth fairy as well.

A dispassionate look at all the many innovations of the insurance industry, from HMOs and managed care to co-pays and prior authorizations, would show that each innovation was a way for insurers to make money at the expense of the public good. If these innovations were studied like a new drug or medical device, they would be taken off the market.

What doctors should be doing as advocates for their patients—as advocates for change—is grading and reviewing the hospitals and insurers, but instead they cower in fear. Doctors get to be doctors by knuckling under, but at some point, for the good of their patients, they should wake up and insist on being in charge.

Both the medical insurers and drug companies make and hold on to as much of the money as they can. They have, to a large extent, subverted the efforts of hospitals and other providers to care for the sick. The sick have been converted into financial instruments whereby large amounts of money are transferred from one corporation to another. The business opportunities presented by sickness and the threat of sickness have cast into outer darkness the opportunity for medical practitioners to be of help and service.

A hundred years ago the Flexner Report revolutionized medical education and medical care by emphasizing science and paying attention to what happened to patients. It's always possible that history will repeat itself. Maybe today's medical students or the next generation or the next will say, "No. This is how it should be done. First, do no harm, care about what happens to patients, and settle arguments with good science."

You Can't Ignore Gravity, 2008

(Painting by Mark Vonnegut)

chapter 13

Short Chapter . . .

Relationships are absurd spindly contrivances
Of Love Lust + Luck
How sad when we see
Of course
It can't work

Three years and two more marriage counselors after Honduras, I hadn't had a drink in five years. I smashed a glass at my wife's feet and broke an expensive tile. The next day I pushed a chair she was in.

I had to leave.

Whatever peace we had managed to work out couldn't survive my not drinking.

My wife and I had both come from damaged, damaging childhoods, and both of us desperately wanted to be normal and thought that being married to each other would be a ticket away from where we didn't want to be. She liked the very un-needy Clint Eastwood–type man I had tried so hard to be. She had bragged to her women's group about how little trouble I was.

Now, suddenly, I was a jumpy mess who needed a drink and couldn't have one. It was embarrassing for both of us that I had gone nuts and thrown those rocks out of the aquarium at her and been hauled off to the hospital in a straightjacket. You can't go from being someone who drinks at least a little bit every day to someone who doesn't drink like it's wearing different clothes and cutting your hair shorter. She was a perfectly okay woman whom I didn't feel loved by. I would have done anything except drink to have my own goddamned feelings matter less.

What possibly could happen to a forty-five-year-old man with two kids that would make getting divorced come out okay?

At my most pathetic, when I felt lost and very sorry for myself and was no longer in charge of making breakfast and packing lunches for my boys, I set up a bird feeder on the ledge of my apartment overlooking a parking lot and no birds came.

End of the Lane, 1991

(Painting by Mark Vonnegut)

Use all the armor.

(Photo by Barb Vonnegut)

chapter 14

The Myth of Mental Wellness

Just 'cause there's nothing wrong with you
doesn't make you right.

Our medical school graduation speaker was a Jesuit psychiatrist who made me laugh and cry at the same time. At least one person in the world understood why I had become a doctor. So I made a mental note, with my two-year-old son, Zach, sitting on my lap, that should I ever need a psychiatrist again, he would be the guy.

I started going to Ned as a patient in the fall of my internship year, right after my sister had a psychotic break that started with voices and not being able to eat or sleep after giving up drinking. At one point she lay down in the aisle of an airplane so that the Black Jesus and White Jesus could talk to each other. I had zero clue drinking was a problem for her. I just thought she was unhappy some of the time because she was married to a jerk.

Harvard's health services had taken me off lithium halfway through my second year, when I discovered during anatomy that my thyroid was enlarged. After an ultrasound and a bunch of blood tests, it was determined that I had benign nodular thyromegaly and that the lithium the "vitamin doctors" had put me on might have something to do with it. I had some unsatisfactory sessions with the medical school shrink, who was annoyingly smug and fatherly. He didn't have a diagnosis for whatever it was that had caused the three psychotic episodes in British Columbia, but going off the lithium was fine with me. I felt pretty much okay and all set forever.

When my sister got sick I hadn't taken lithium for two years and my thyroid was still three times its normal size and lumpy. I was shaken and upset because no one else in my family seemed to be able to get it together to deal with anything and because there were too many dead-ringer parallels between my sister's psychosis and mine and I still had no name for whatever it was I had. This was in 1979, eight years after my initial episodes. How could I be so sure I was finished with it if I didn't know what it was?

I was the model of efficiency helping my sister in New York, at least partly because I was looking forward to telling Ned how it went.

I don't tell Ned everything. The truth about the voices, my grandiosity, and flights of ideas would just upset him. He might feel the need to do something about them, and it would take more time than I have to reassure him that I'm really all right.

NED: "So what about thinking that people don't know who you really are or that the radio is talking about you or to you?"

ME: "Not me, boss."

The truth about the voices is that once you've heard them, they are always there, just more or less offstage and more or less intelligible. Once you've been talked to by voices, it's not possible to go back to a world where talking to voices is not possible. Having been crazy, I know that God can, if He wants, run me like a toy train.

NED: "Do you ever ask God to help you with a diagnosis?"

ME: "No."

I actually had tried that and found out that physical diagnosis wasn't one of God's strengths. To be precise, what He said was, "Why do you think I created Harvard? I wouldn't have bothered to send you to medical school if I knew you were going to come back to me with questions about physical diagnosis. You already know the patient doesn't have appendicitis. Don't bother me with crap like this again."

"But..."

So if I'm really so all right, why do I go see a psychiatrist at all?

Over the years I've come to care about Ned, and I think I go mostly to make sure he's okay. He comforts me about my increasingly balky memory and moodiness by assuring me that his memory and tendency to fly off the handle are worse than mine. It works for me.

I still consider myself an early-Christianity scholar on a spiritual quest that happened to lead to medical school. Ned and I don't talk much about early Christianity, but we could. I have a problem with Saint Paul, who never actually met Jesus, and with whoever it was who wrote the book of Revelation (it was definitely not Saint John). I also take issue with the idea that Jesus, after the Crucifixion and Resurrection, started working out and riding horses and having second thoughts about the Sermon on the Mount and the beatitudes. Where did this new muscular Christ come from? What are the four horsemen of the apocalypse so pissed about? What situation could possibly be made better by unleashing war, pestilence, famine, and death?

✷

Passing for normal hasn't been a problem for me for a while now. I know how to dress and act and how to not exactly tell the truth about what's going on. I could pass off the things that happened to me when I was crazy as just a bunch of craziness, but the problem is, when I'm trying my best to tell the truth to myself, I'm not sure I didn't bargain God down from nuclear cataclysm to a relatively mild earthquake and stop my father from killing himself. I'm glad I got to meet and talk to Dostoyevsky, van Gogh, Beethoven, Freud, and Abraham Lincoln and continue to count them as good friends.

✷

There was one thing I was very sure of in early sobriety, and that was that I shouldn't talk to the woman who casually complimented my haircut one day. I knew that my friend Max knew her phone number—he owned the apartment she was living in—and I didn't want not having her phone number to be the reason I wasn't calling her. You have to wake up very early if you want to try to outthink me.

We had had a few tentative dates after we were recruited to help out an underpowered softball team. I think it was the IT-support department of Boston University. I was coaching first base, and she hit a solid line drive in the gap between right and center field, so when she got to first I told her to go to second. She stopped dead in her tracks, turned to me, and said, "Don't tell me what to do."

We were married six years later.

It hasn't escaped Barb that I go to my psychiatrist mostly to see how he's doing. She's not sure I shouldn't see someone else.

"They'd have problems too," I point out. "Then I'd have two psychiatrists to worry about."

∗

The difference between me and crazy people who have not done well is *not much.* Melville Weston Fuller Wallace III was one of my mother's favorite friends of mine. We met working together at a restaurant when we were both seventeen. He lived mostly at our house one summer, and one of my sisters had a crush on him. One Fourth of July when I was nineteen I was visiting with him at his parents' New York apartment. I had had too much to drink, and he was shushing me and taking care of me. He was no more or less schizophrenic than I was, but that's his current diagnosis. He was a pretty good painter and a pretty good musician. I had my first episode three years later. He had his a year after that, when he was twenty-three. He and I have both been married twice. He's homeless now and writes me heartbreakingly difficult-to-decipher letters and sends me beautiful geometric watercolors.

I went looking for him once in L.A., along the Santa Monica boardwalk. It had been so long since I had seen Fuller that I had no idea what he might look like. I talked to about twenty people who might have been Fuller, and many of them thought they probably knew who I was talking about, but no one was sure. I showed them his paintings and said that he played the flute.

Things do not even out.

∗

There are no people anywhere who don't have some mental illness. It all depends on where you set the bar and how hard you look. What is a myth is that we are mostly mentally well most of the time.

The bad behavior of others constitutes an attractive nuisance to someone recovering from mental illness. You need all your energy and wits for things that matter. Beyond a certain point, gathering further evidence of the hurtfulness and shortcomings of one's family, employer, et cetera is like eating the same poisonous mushroom over and over and expecting that sooner or later it will be nutritious.

If recovery from mental illness depended on the goodness, mercy, and rational behavior of others, we'd all be screwed. Peace of mind is inversely proportional to expectations.

It's possible within any given moment of any given day to choose between self and sickness. Rarely are there big heroic choices that will settle matters once and for all. The smallest positive step is probably the right one. Try not to argue. If you're right, you don't need to argue. If you're wrong, it won't help. If you're okay, things will be okay. If you're not okay, nothing else matters.

A world without prejudice, stigma, and discrimination against those who have or who are thought to have mental illness would be a better world for everyone. What so-called normal people are doing when they define disease like manic depression or schizophrenia is reassuring themselves that they don't have a thought disorder or affective disorder, that their thoughts and feelings make perfect sense.

There's a Path, 1999

(Painting by Mark Vonnegut)

Honeymoon

(Photo by innocent bystander)

chapter 15

Bricks and Lobsters

If you need a drink, have one before the ceremony.
We won't have any alcohol at the house. We took all the
money and blew it on soft-shelled crabs, oysters, and barbeque.
—our wedding invitation

There had been fourteen years between my third and fourth breaks. Fourteen years after the fourth break I was very relieved that nothing untoward seemed to be happening in my head. Barb, who I knew was trouble the minute I saw her, and I decided to get married after five years together. We bought a two-hundred-year-old barn and carriage house with major structural issues and a lot wrong with the rest of it too. More sensible people would have torn it down and started over.

When I was telling a neighbor what he could do with a big maple tree that was dying—make planks out of the trunk, use the smaller branches for firewood and the scraps for kindling, plus the sawdust could be mixed with compost and used to grow mushrooms—my wife said I sounded like a male version of Martha Stewart.

It's more about *Doctor Zhivago*. If I'm careful to not waste things, especially things that have to do with heat and staying warm, I'll never have to go out in a blizzard and come home with a few pathetic pieces of pine ripped out of a fence.

Trash costs three dollars a barrel to remove. All the landfills are closed, and you can't get rid of a pickup-truck-load of brush for less than $150.

When Omar Sharif went out into the freezing Russian winter to search for fuel to keep his sickly, starving wife and child from freezing to death, he came back with three ¾-inch boards of plain pine, the combined caloric content of which was probably less than what he wasted opening and closing the door. Taking into account the high ceilings and inefficient stove, it probably wasn't a net gain.

But it wasn't nothing. He couldn't have known that those boards were what he was going to find. At least he came back with something, but if he had come back with three or four dry oak logs and had an airtight stove, it would have been a whole different story. It was really just a plot device, a way for him to meet his brother, Alec Guinness.

I don't want to throw away building scraps and then need kindling and not have any.

I've had people of questionable immigration status tell me in broken English that *el doctor* shouldn't be burning building scraps for heat.

"Have you ever seen *Doctor Zhivago*? *El Doctor Zhivago?*" They look back blankly.

Bogden was one of my workers who actually had a visa; it was a student visa but a visa nonetheless. Bogden was Polish, the brother of an old girlfriend of Ralph's. Ralph was a carpenter who agreed to help me out with projects and teach me some carpentry as long as I never called him or yelled at him for not getting things done.

Bogden is worse off than the Spanish-speaking guys because no one learns Polish in high school. The deal with Bogden was that Ralph would bring him to our house in the morning and he would work like a bull for ten dollars an hour until you didn't have anything more for him to do. You could drop him at any T station and he'd find his way home.

The first few jobs I gave Bogden were ripping out brush and hauling piles of heavy things from one place to another. It was hard to keep up with him. An overgrown tennis court was turned into something you could almost play on. The tools were lined up like punctuation marks whenever a job was done.

I was making a little brick patio in my backyard.

"Wooooden hammer?" Bogden said, watching me bang bricks into place with other bricks, chipping both the banged and the banger brick.

"Yes. A wooden hammer would be nice, but I don't have one." I actually did have a wooden hammer, but I didn't know where it was.

"Oh. Too bad," said Bogden.

"When you're done sweeping off the tennis court and getting all the stone dust out of the truck, maybe you would like to try the bricks? Does Bogden know bricks?"

"Try bricks? . . . Sure."

When I got back from an afternoon of pediatrics, Ralph had picked up Bogden. The tools were neatly lined up: brush hook, mattock, rake, pitchfork, and my wooden hammer—God knows how he found it. The small terrace I had been struggling with was laid out perfectly. It was level and the joints were tight.

It looked like it had been there for a hundred years. Bogden knew bricks. I started ripping up most of what I had done before to redo it.

Barb took Bogden to the T that night and came back telling me that he was an engineer but that there wasn't much work for engineers in Poland. He was not married but had a girlfriend. I could have worked with him all day every day for months and not figured out that stuff.

"He said that in Poland everybody knows bricks. And then he said, 'Shouldn't it be "In Poland everybody knows *about* bricks"?'"

Since I took up carpentry I measure children much more carefully, sometimes to ⅟₃₂ of an inch.

✳

I have a thing about Russia and Russians. In a past life I was beaten and left to die by the Cossacks or Stalin's goons. My hovel has been burned. I have no idea where my family is. Three of my children died from diphtheria the spring before. The birches have new leaves. It is snowing. I cry tears of joy.

Nikolai is a good man with a good heart and was very much trying to do something nice for us by taking Barb and me and our son out on one of his charter boats. He knew that I loved boats and didn't have one and loved to fish but didn't get to go fishing often. He appreciated that I was honest and available and worked hard at being a good doctor to his kids. I didn't give him a hard time about not wanting to immunize his children. I believe very much in immunization but don't see it as a deal breaker. The less arguing I do about it, the more likely the kids will end up immunized.

"The children of irrational parents need good doctors too, Nikolai," I said. He liked that.

After catching some cod, two bluefish, and an undersized striped bass that we threw back, Nickolai wanted to dive for some lobsters before calling it a day. We anchored a hundred yards off of a beautiful little island that's been proposed as a liquefied natural gas terminal and watched Nikolai's bubbles. He was down there a half hour and came up out of breath with three mesh bags full of lobsters.

Understanding favors in a second language isn't always easy.

I'm sure he would have preferred that they were bigger. There were twenty-three very small lobsters. The biggest one was maybe six inches long. They were basically big crawfish. He wouldn't have had to stay under so long if they'd been bigger. I was encouraged when he checked the undersides for eggs and threw one back.

We had talked earlier about declining fish stocks, and he had said, "Fishermen cannot catch so many fish to deplete. If are not enough fish, is chemicals and pollution from too many people." I agreed.

Nikolai grew up in Siberia the son of some of the "fewer but better Russians" Stalin talked about when asked if he felt bad about the purges. He had big hands and was muscular but small and thin in a way that spoke of caloric deprivation either of his mother during her pregnancy or of him early in his infancy, maybe both. He was about five feet four inches tall. You could pour all the calories you liked into Nikolai, and they would never stick. Born in a different place and time, he would have been well over six feet tall. If they keep growing at their current percentiles, his son will tower over him and his daughter will be roughly his height.

Fishing charters was only one of the things Nikolai was up to. He was a mechanic and engineer working on a better way to start bio-diesel engines. It made sense to me. I've never known a Russian who was up to just one thing.

I asked a little nervously about measuring the lobsters.

"Are better this way. Only measure these lobsters need is on the fork in your mouth."

Someone who had grown up starving in Siberia could be forgiven a different attitude toward what you should and shouldn't eat, but I'd been arrested before for taking quahogs that were allegedly too small and knew how humorless and difficult resource-conservation officers could be. And the lobsters were really tiny. I wondered what my wife was making of all this. She seemed to be in endurance mode, unusually quiet.

I tried to divide them into a pile for my family—three or four—and a pile for his family—all the rest.

"I never eat them," he explained succinctly. "Kids and wife don't like them either."

They were all for us.

I could just see the cop who might stop us doing a double take before opening the cooler. "Any relation to Kurt? Aren't you a pediatrician? Didn't you do some ads for Blue Cross?"

Maybe there was a fine of a thousand dollars apiece for possessing lobsters this small, maybe there wasn't. I didn't know for sure but would have supported such a law. What possible excuse could there be for riding around with a cooler nearly full of cod and bluefish topped off with twenty-plus tiny lobsters?

I'd bake some of the cod for dinner. Whatever cod we didn't eat that night could be frozen. The bluefish I could smoke. Nikolai had put little rubber bands on each of the lobsters' claws so they wouldn't tear one another apart in the close quarters of the cooler.

We had gone on the trip expecting a two- or three-hour deal that had turned into seven. Our three-year-old had held up well. It would be good to get home. We said our goodbyes. With the cooler in the back of the pickup truck, I readjusted my mirrors and drove very carefully, not too fast, not too slow, no U-turns. Our son fell asleep instantly. The truck was very quiet.

A few minutes into our trip home I looked over at my wife. "We've got to try to let the lobsters go."

"Do you think they can live?" They'd been on ice but out of water a couple of hours.

"They're alive now. We have to give them a chance."

The only place I could think of with deep-enough water was a popular fishing dock. Lugging a cooler down the dock and liberating baby lobsters might attract attention. I'd have to get all those rubber bands off—a chance at life with banded claws wasn't much of a chance. We'd stick out like a whole hand of sore thumbs throwing lobsters out of a cooler on a fishing dock. *Sure there's a Russian fisherman....*

If there had been one or even two or three of them, it wouldn't have been so bad. The large number spoke to callous indifference and criminal intent.

I don't stick out. I'm exactly average height, an average amount overweight, with brown hair and brown eyes. I worry about being in the wrong place at the wrong time or not having the right identification. The thought of being caught with these lobsters was almost worse than death itself.

"I think there's some pretty deep water off a breakwater down behind a car dealership in Weymouth."

We found the parking lot and watched in silence for a few minutes to see if anyone was around. I climbed halfway down the breakwater dragging the cooler, slightly twisting an ankle before I could find a place to steady it and myself. One by one I took off the bands and threw the lobsters into the water. I could see them lying there, not moving, for a while, but then they jerked around and seemed to recover.

I knew from having found lobsters in marsh pools while quahogging that they don't need a lot of water. They were less than a hundred yards from Quincy Bay, where there were lots of other lobsters, but if this was the end of the line, at least they had one another. We were out of there.

"I think that they're okay, but maybe I should have given them one of the bluefish," I told my wife as I got into the truck. Our three-year-old was dead to the world, asleep, strapped into his car seat. "I'm going to tell Nikolai that they were the best lobsters we ever ate."

The world that went forward from that moment was a world where we, at some small—but not zero—risk to ourselves, set free twenty-three small lobsters somewhere off a parking lot in Weymouth rather than eating them, which would have been the easier thing to do.

We are saltwater ocean people.

(Photo by M. Oliver Vonnegut)

Never lie down with your children
to get them to sleep.

(Photo by Barb Vonnegut)

chapter 16

The Rope

Don't just do something. Stand there.
—Dr. Elvin Semrad

The grandfather of a thirteen-year-old boy I'd taken care of since he was a baby asked if he could talk to me before I saw his grandson.

"His mother hung herself last Friday."

The grandfather was bringing up the boy because the mother, whom I had never met, couldn't stop drinking.

"Was she ever able to get any sobriety? Was she ever able to take care of him?" I asked.

"Not really. It's probably a blessing for her that it's over." He never mentioned that the mother his grandson had just lost was his daughter.

The boy was very small and said to be retarded because of fetal alcohol syndrome. As soon as I figure out what you should say to a thirteen-year-old boy whose mother has just hung herself, I'll let you know.

"I'm sorry about your mom."

"................................."

"Alcoholism is a terrible disease."

"..................................."

"It's a terrible disease that killed your mother."

"Yeah, Doc. That and the rope around her neck."

Prescribing a pill is far and away the quickest way to bring closure to a patient encounter. No prescription hangs in the air begging. Often the patient says, "So, are we done?"

I had no pills for the boy with the hung mother.

I spent much of my childhood worried that Kurt would kill himself. Whether or not I'd be ready to lose my father was something I had started asking myself almost as soon as I knew there was such a thing as death. From time to time, in an almost conversational tone, he mentioned that he might commit suicide. There didn't seem to be much anguish involved. My mother was understandably preoccupied with whether or not my father might kill himself. She believed more than he did that he would someday be a famous writer, and she promoted and clung to that belief as a way to make sure that he didn't kill himself. His mother had allegedly killed herself. I say *allegedly* because not everyone thought so and I wanted that doubt to lessen the chances of my father doing the same.

✳

My father had thick, dark, curly hair right up until the end. When gray started to creep in he was nearly eighty. I thought maybe he was having gray highlights put in so people would stop mentioning how thick and black his hair was.

No one is going to look at me and say, "Look at the bald

guy," but I have less hair than I used to. When I saw a circular little bit of shiny skin showing through the top back of my head in a photo, I thought there must be some mistake, that the light must have hit my head in a certain way and made it look like a bald spot.

Once upon a time, my hair was not only thick but halfway down my back as well. I'm not sure my hair would even grow that long anymore. It gets lonely and wispy a few inches from my scalp. I used to have *hair.* Now I have these here and those over there. When I was younger, one place on my head was pretty much like any other. I've had more than my share of hair but had hoped for more than just being able to pass for not bald.

I wasn't really accusing my barber of anything when I mentioned the "indicator strip." I had suspected for some time that the hairs just to the left of the middle part became annoyingly long and unmanageable four or five weeks after a haircut so I would know I was supposed to go back and get another one. I thought it might be a small trade secret and was curious to see what Al would say about it.

Al had been cutting my hair for years, but he and I didn't usually talk much. The lack of mandatory chatting is something I value in a barbershop. People do talk there. It's banter about sports mostly, but if you don't want to, you don't have to talk. I tried some more upscale places to get my hair cut a long time ago, but even when I had an appointment and was on time there was something awkward about how I came through the door or checked in or said I had an appointment that led to my sitting awhile listening to the snipping and whispering while easier, more graceful people got their hair cut.

There's no whispering at my barbershop. Al couldn't whisper on a bet. We'd had some conversations before, actually more like contests to see if we could remember the same things about old Red Sox teams and Elvis Presley.

We talk more now, and what broke the dam was my asking him if he deliberately leaves a lock of hair just to the right of my part that becomes unmanageable four or five weeks after a haircut so I know when I'm supposed to come back.

He was a little surprised.

"Not really. We don't leave an indicator strip or anything like that," he said after a pause, during which he just stood there with scissors and comb in his hand. I thought that that would be the end of it, but then he started talking. "This is really a Dorchester haircut I'm giving you, not a Hyde Park haircut at all. Your hair is thinning on top. Not bad. But it's less noticeable if I leave a little more on the sides and shape it down. When you have a lot of hair it doesn't really matter how you cut it." He has a toupee.

We both agree that being in good health and looking good for guys in our sixties is better than the alternative, but that what we really want is to look good and be nineteen.

✳

There was something wrong with me besides hearing voices and jumping through windows, besides schizophrenia or manic depression or schizoaffective disorder. What was wrong with me was that I couldn't love or accept love.

Besides that, Mrs. Lincoln, how was the play?

It seemed unfair that someone who worked as hard as I did to be right about so many things should be unloved. There were people who liked me or seemed to like me, but what if I wasn't a doctor, hadn't published a book, wasn't Kurt Vonnegut's son? The truth is, I was terrified and wouldn't have trusted or accepted love if it came and sat in my lap—*especially* if it came and sat in my lap. I didn't have the faintest idea who I was. Publishing a book, getting into medical school, and getting to be a pretty good doctor saved my life and kept me barely alive, but by the time I went crazy for the fourth and, I hope, last time, my soul was on life support.

I had a prayer that went, "God, whatever I am, let it be for good." By my mid-thirties it had morphed into "God, what the f—— am I?"

Now I'm sixty-two. My first child is thirty-two. His son is walking and talking. If you don't want to miss life, don't blink. Somehow having my awesome willpower come up short against alcohol got rid of the three-inch-thick Plexiglas separating me from the rest of the world. I can now love and accept love.

※

I get to see people at their best. No one wants to be a lousy parent. I've seen hopeless narcissists become good parents and stop being narcissists. I didn't think that was possible.

The best parents are poor people who have a little bit of money and rich people who have had a little bit of poverty.

※

By the time he is twelve years old the average child has heard about drugs, alcohol, and unsafe sex so often that the messages are blocked before reaching consciousness. He has also been told over and over that if he works hard and gets good grades things will go well for him, which is a lie. Drugs are a way to be dead but just for a little while.

I find I can sometimes break through the glaze of boredom by saying things like "If you're having trouble making decisions, maybe you should smoke a lot of marijuana." Or "The great thing about not having a drinking problem is that you can drink yourself into a blackout whenever you like." Or "Safe sex is better than no sex at all." These can lead to useful conversations.

＊

All you have to know about the power of will and choice is that most drug addicts can't stop, even when they want to.

＊

Not infrequently, a boy will hand me a cup of pee that couldn't have come from him because there are vaginal cells in it or signs of a period or a urinary tract infection. The first sign of something wrong is often that the temperature of the pee is closer to room temperature than to 98.6. Another clue is when the person being tested tells his parent that he'll go wait for them in the car.

"Go get John. I have to talk to him," I say.

The parent knows better than to ask why and retrieves the invariably bristling, sullen "What is up with this lame doctor?" patient.

"It's not your pee," I say.

"It's not my pee?" Shock, outrage, and denial.

"It's not your pee." This can go on for a while.

"How can you tell?"

"It's too cold. And it came from a girl. If your parents think you need a drug test and you can't beat the test with someone else's pee, you don't have a gift for getting away with things."

"Are you going to tell my parents?"

"No, you are. I'd rather not deal with your parents directly.

The only reason for me to test your urine for drugs is to help you stay clean when you've decided that's what you want. The fact that you're fifteen years old trying to pass off someone else's urine as your own means to me that marijuana is probably not your friend and might get in the way of whatever else it is you want your life to be about. Did you pay for this pee or was it from a friend?"

On the Internet you can buy fake pee to pass drug tests that comes in a realistic penis container so that when the test is strictly monitored, which means someone is in the bathroom with you and watches the pee go into the cup, you can squeeze the pee into a cup from the fake penis.

I don't monitor my patients giving urine, mostly because my job is hard enough without hanging out in bathrooms with adolescents who are trying to pee. Partly I'm trying to give them a shred of privacy and dignity, and partly I'm curious as to whether, given the chance, they'll try to give me someone else's pee. Catching them at it, especially early in the process, especially when I'm not really trying, has led to conversations in which the patient actually ends up caring about whether or not he does drugs. Sometimes.

When the urine drug screens I send out are negative, sometimes it's even because the patient involved isn't doing drugs. Consider all the possibilities.

If I see someone and I don't recognize him because all the softness and pinkness has melted out of his face, I assume he's doing drugs. Addictive drugs take all your little problems, like having a difficult family or feeling insecure, and trade them in for one big problem, having to have drugs. Childhood isn't fun for everyone. One of the attractive things about drugs is that they give children a way to stop being a child. Bye-bye pain and fear; hello addiction.

If there is a last judgment, if there's an outside chance of a last judgment, do you want to be standing there with someone else's pee?

Parents tend to think that a negative or positive drug test accomplishes more than it possibly can. If their child has clean urine, all is not necessarily well. If the test is positive, very few children, confronted with proof of drug usage, will stop. They can't. I care about the results of the drug test, but the real goal is for the child to have a life that doesn't involve being in my office, handing me a cup of urine that might not be his.

A positive drug test is an opportunity for collaboration. If we can't come up with clean urine, we're going to have to keep doing tests that cost money and take valuable time out of our day. The easiest way to come up with negative drug tests is to stop doing drugs, but it goes better if you let the child think of that on his own. Then not doing drugs is no longer a moral issue but a practical, cost-effective way to deal with the annoying problem of having illegal drugs in your urine.

"Hey, Jack, this is Dr. Vonnegut. I've got some good news and some bad news. There's no more THC in your urine and that's great, but now there are some cocaine metabolites in there."

"I wonder how those got in there?"

"I don't know, Jack, maybe you left the window open or something, but now we have to do another test. Cocaine is a whole different deal. Are you still talking to Frank? Going to those meetings? Do you want to come in and talk to me about it or just go over to the lab and pee?"

Most of life is a soggy mess, but you can make the world a very different place. As hard as addiction is, it's always possible to quit and change your perception of the world from one where you do drugs and just about nothing good is possible to one where you don't do drugs and good things can happen.

Twenty-five years ago, when I had a patient with a drug problem it was a big deal. I called people and they returned my calls and my patients got treatment. Treatment doesn't exist now, not because it wasn't effective, but because it's less expensive for insurers to let addicts and their families drift into poverty and join the ranks of the uninsured.

If not helping a fourteen-year-old addict won't come back and bite us in the ass, what will?

"It's not your pee. And if you weren't doing drugs that woman over there who is crying and has been calling me on the phone so much, your mother, wouldn't have brought you to my office to hand me someone else's pee that you had to secretly cradle the whole car ride over."

∗

My generation should be given credit for proving beyond all shadow of a doubt that drugs are bad for you.

Dad, 2004

(Painting by Mark Vonnegut)

chapter 17

There's Nothing Quite as Final as a Dead Father

We do, doodily do, doodily do, doodily do
what we must, muddily must, muddily must, muddily must,
    muddily do, muddily do, muddily do, muddily do,
until we bust, bodily bust, bodily bust, bodily bust.
—Kurt Vonnegut, Jr. (1922–2007)

Kurt was more like an unpredictable younger brother who refused to grow up than a father. He was a wonderful writer and
capable of great warmth and kindness, but he fiercely defended
and exercised his right to be a pain in the ass on a regular basis.

My last gift to him was a complete bust. He was a famous
Luddite who refused to use email or have anything to do with
word processors till the very end. So when I came across a manual Olivetti typewriter on eBay that looked exactly like the one
on which he had typed most of his novels, I thought he might
want to hang it on the wall like a piece of art or the head of an
animal he had hunted. I was not suggesting he return to writing.

It was supposed to be for his eighty-fourth birthday. He wasn't exactly easy to shop for.

When I opened the package, the typewriter was in horrible shape and had a script typeface, which I was sure Kurt would make fun of. I started searching harder and found that Olivetti made a modern manual typewriter. I ordered one and, because time was short, requested that it be shipped directly to his house, but then they put it on back order, and it wouldn't be delivered till a month after his birthday. So I canceled the order, but somehow it didn't die and a huge, heavy crate arrived at my father's door two months after his birthday.

"It's the size of a goddamned switch engine. I don't want it. I'm done writing. What do I want with another GD typewriter?" he said. *What kind of an idiot would send me a typewriter?* was the barely unspoken message.

"I canceled the order a long time ago. Let me get Eli to come over and move the damn thing for you. The idea was to appreciate it as a machine and maybe put it on the wall. I had no idea it would be so big. It certainly wasn't to make you write again. It was a lousy idea. I'm sorry," I said. *Cut your son a little slack.*

Part of me wanted to have a real switch engine delivered to his door for comparison.

✻

My twenty-five-year-old son and his wife and my wife and our four-year-old were in New York City in our hotel, thinking of easy places to take Kurt for dinner. When I called him and offered him some choices, he said he didn't want to go out. So maybe we'd just come over and Eli and his wife and the rest of us could say hello before we went out. But it turned out that Kurt wanted to see me but nobody else. He was eighty-four so we cut him some slack, but the truth is we'd been cutting Kurt slack for forever. He'd been just as capable of being unreasonable and ungracious when he was fifty-four. So because I'm a saint and a martyr and didn't know how else to be a good fifty-nine-year-old son, I hobbled crosstown on crutches since I couldn't find a cab and the traffic was bad. He left the door open and came toward me but barely looked at me when I let myself in.

He'd been arguing with his wife, Jill, which was maybe why he was in such a lousy mood. She stayed in the kitchen and didn't greet me.

He'd been thinking about the right-wing religious groups who were so into the Ten Commandments and wondered why they weren't into the beatitudes.

I proposed that they were picking a fight and practicing being an angry mob. The reason the Democrats lost Florida in 2000 was that the Republicans had the better-drilled, better-armed, and more-prepared-to-fight mob. Most individual members of the mob, so eager to have plaques of the Ten Commandments in courthouses, couldn't name more than three of them.

I liked, a little too much, that he thought I might be right. At the age of fifty-nine, hobbling across Manhattan on crutches for conditional approval from my father was okay with me.

His wife came into the living room and picked a fight about whether their adopted daughter, Lily, should be made to take her medicine. She appealed to my expertise as a pediatrician.

I asked what Lily, who was then already in her twenties, liked to do and whether or not she thought the medication might help her on her own terms. Jill said something else. Kurt said that if this discussion continued he would leave. Jill continued calling

Kurt irresponsible. Kurt fled upstairs, holding his head and wearing the facial expression of someone in hell in a Hieronymus Bosch painting. Jill complained about Kurt fleeing. Kurt came back downstairs and talked about how Bush should be impeached.

I counted it as a good visit and took a cab back to my family in Times Square.

There were a few more phone calls, but that was our last visit. He left me with the blessing of things to do for him, like being his medical proxy. It fell to me to be the one with him in his last days. I played music and told jokes I thought he'd like.

"If this doesn't wake him up, he's not waking up."

He didn't wake up. I was able to enforce some elements of decorum around his deathbed. His suffering was not dragged out. Without me acting as his proxy, no one wanted to be responsible for the death of an icon. He was not shipped to a futile neuro-rehab in New Jersey.

So I took care of my father like my father had cut through the crap and taken care of me thirty-six years earlier in British Columbia. I was glad to be able to repay the favor. He took responsibility for hospitalizing me, and I took responsibility for letting him go.

✳

My father gave me the gifts of being able to pay attention to my inner narration no matter how tedious the damn thing could be at times and the knowledge that creating something, be it music or a painting or a poem or a short story, was a way out of wherever you were and a way to find out what the hell happens next and not have it be just the same old thing. It's better to live in a world where you can write and paint and tell a few jokes than one where you can't.

All the arts are ways to start a dialogue with yourself about what you've done, what you could have done differently, and whether or not you might try again. Whether or not you want to make a living or can make a living at it, people who consistently bother to try almost always get good or at least better.

Kurt was always trying to reach a little beyond what he was sure of. His refusal to find a groove and stay there when he was famous and successful was admirable, but it was also because he dreaded what life would be if he stopped being creative, honest, and willing to be awkward.

※

So one month short of my sixtieth birthday I became an orphan. I had lost my mother twenty years earlier. I was no longer on deck. There's nothing quite as final as a dead father.

Right after the memorial service, my good friend Terry and I were in Times Square with our backs against a wall, watching the sea of humanity surge by. Terry asked why I was smiling.

"I'm just watching all these people who have made something out of nothing."

A day at the beach

(Photo by Barb Vonnegut)

chapter 18

Mushrooms

Since I always do what I always do, I must be doing it again.

I started hunting wild mushrooms when I was allowed to get up and move around after an operation to save my left eye, a consequence of the twenty-seven-inning August softball madness. My retina detached in protest of my being dehydrated and fifty-two and running around crashing into people. That was the year after I shattered two bones in my hand. It was like I couldn't take a hint. A week after the operation I was allowed up and could walk around but was supposed to only look down. So I became a hunter of wild mushrooms.

When they were drawing up the medicines to keep me quiet for the operation, and I'd been twelve years without a drink or a drug, I knew the little syringe was fentanyl, a very pure, highly addictive narcotic.

"How much do you weigh?"

"Three hundred twenty-seven pounds."

"You carry it well."

I was surprised that I didn't enjoy it more. It was sort of bright and giggly, but I felt like I was being made to stay inside and watch cartoons on a sunny day when I wanted to go out and play. It didn't help being in a hospital and knowing they were poking and cutting my eye, and that I had just signed a piece of paper that said I knew I might go blind.

When I needed operations on my knees the orthopedist offered me the option of doing it under local anesthesia.

"You're kidding, right?"

I was looking forward to being unconscious.

There's a moment right after you swallow the first bite of a new mushroom that you are 99+ percent sure is okay when the less-than-1 percent chance that it's not looms large. There's a halo of attention around eating a new mushroom that can last for days.

On a spring walk with my dog, Ella, I noticed a dozen or so black morel mushrooms under a tree in the yard of a house about a mile from ours. There was a car in the driveway and a light on. Before I knew what I was doing, I was gathering up the mushrooms and stuffing them into my pockets and the dog-poop bag I usually bring along. My dog was whining and looking around nervously. Like she doesn't cause me plenty of embarrassment pooping wherever she likes, chasing after other dogs.

I could have come back at night. What if the people at home looked out and maybe even recognized me? Maybe I was even their pediatrician? Whether you know the people or not, knocking on their door to ask if you can take mushrooms they probably didn't know were there seems too strange. I grabbed the mushrooms and took off quickly but not so quickly as to attract attention. I found several more morels on my way home. They were delicious.

Once you've risked death or social embarrassment by eating something and it tastes good, it strongly rewards all the steps that went before so that time, place, shape, color, and weather all acquire richness and meaning.

> It is much more important to not eat a poisonous mushroom than it is to eat an edible one.
> —David Arora, *Mushrooms Demystified*

I read the sentence over and over. I can't figure out exactly where the error lies.

"I think I'm getting the hang of it," said my wife, picking up another mushroom. This was prior to the *unfortunate incident*. I was gratified that she was taking an interest in my hobby. You can spend a lifetime not seeing mushrooms, but once you see them, you will always see them. It's not something you can just stop. Seeing mushrooms takes place somewhere between the brain stem and the cortex. My head will snap around sometimes when I'm driving, and I'll realize that I must have seen something that looked like a mushroom and I wonder which one.

Once you notice mushrooms, it's hard to not want to do something about them, even if it's only to know what their name is. But eventually knowing about them leads to eating them. I was surprised to read descriptions of the smell, texture, and taste of some of the most thoroughly unappealing, unappetizing, and even deadly poisonous mushrooms. There are some very dedicated people, a good deal crazier than me, walking around the woods. If I was going to put my life and bodily organs at risk, it was only going to be for something that tasted really good.

The porcini or cep mushroom, *Boletus edulis,* is at or very near the top of everyone's list. They can grow up to a foot across and weigh more than two pounds, and they are virtually impossible to confuse with any poisonous mushrooms. Prior to the *unfortunate incident,* I found, cooked, and ate many very good-tasting mushrooms, some of them rated almost as good as *Boletus edulis,* and I found a few that might have been the porcini. I couldn't be sure because they were well past their prime and most of the way back to being dust.

Wild mushrooms spring up overnight and are fit for eating for a day or two, three at the most.

There's a house in my neighborhood with surveillance cameras and warning signs and big black Lincolns that come and go. The house is set way back and the lawn is huge. What if there were porcini mushrooms growing on that lawn? Would I black my face and come back in the wee hours? Could I train my dog to fetch mushrooms? Were those cameras real? Did the people in the house have a sense of humor? Did they like mushrooms? If it was a Mafia guy, maybe he remembered porcini mushrooms from his childhood and I'd be in the position of having to be damn sure and cooking them just right, hoping against hope they weren't the bitter boletes. Bitter boletes aren't poisonous, but they look like porcini and taste horrible. The Mafia guy would be trying to spit this bitter taste out of his mouth. "Porcini, my ass." And I'd be going for a ride somewhere.

Collecting mushrooms sounds so gentlemanly.

While they say there are no surefire ways to identify poisonous mushrooms, avoiding the ones that glow in the dark and smell like death seems like a safe practice. Yet there are mushrooms that smell like rotting fish that cook up nicely. The fact that some of the very poisonous amanitas taste good goes against much of what I hoped to be true about life. I imagine some poor, fatally poisoned SOB talking to fellow mushroom collectors on his deathbed. "At first I didn't think it tasted like much, but then..."

Ever since taking me to have my stomach pumped, Barb has had a negative attitude toward my fascination with mushrooms. I've explained to her that the mushroom I ingested only rarely causes fatalities and then it is usually in older debilitated people with kidney or liver failure. Debilitated older people with kidney or liver failure have no business eating wild mushrooms unless they are utterly and completely sure of their identification.

In the interest of being helpful I tried to give a neighbor some information about some edible mushrooms growing in his yard. "Sautée them in butter and a little garlic salt," I offered. He was polite enough but didn't seem likely to take personal advantage of his good luck. Nor did he offer to let me pick them.

When you walk through the woods, how much of the living matter there is animal, including bugs and birds and all? Two to three percent. Plants, trees, bushes, moss, grass, and flowers—most of what you see and think of when you think of a walk in the woods—make up 15 to 20 percent, depending. The rest is all a very quiet, nearly invisible world of fungi. The mushrooms you see aren't so much the tip of the iceberg as dewdrops on top of the ocean.

The mushroom growing out of my neighbor's stump was the

Armillaria mellea or honey mushroom, so called because of its honey color rather than a sweet honey taste. *Armillaria* is in many ways the most successful organism on the planet. While most mushrooms are recyclers that break down dead or dying plants and return the raw materials to the earth, the honey mushroom will take down perfectly healthy trees and sometimes an entire forest. Most of the organism consists of small black cords that travel miles and miles and miles. The mushrooms you see are the flower of a much much bigger organism. There's a single *Armillaria* that covers most of Oregon and some of northern California. In Europe there's an *Armillaria* that stretches from Tuscany to just outside of Barcelona.

I don't want to make people worry and it seems on the face of it wrong to conceive of a mushroom as having intent, but it makes basic good sense to be careful about being too sure what a thousand-mile-long, three-billion-ton, contiguous, ten-thousand-year-old organism that eats forests and can cross mountains and rivers is and isn't up to.

Mushrooms have six genders, one that is sort of male, two that are sort of female, and three that are something else.

Straight-out without a lot of qualifiers, I should admit that I am not a careful person. The fact that I have managed to achieve certain things doesn't matter. That I am aware of my uncarefulness isn't as helpful as you might think. My parents were told by the principal of West Barnstable Elementary School and my teacher that I was a bright boy whose spelling was in the retarded range and whose handwriting was the worst they'd ever seen. I find it embarrassing that I spell so badly. I will do almost anything to avoid being embarrassed, but no effort either on my part or on the part of any teacher has ever dented my utter bafflement when it comes to choosing which letters to put down, how many, and in what order.

Somewhere in high school I came across Mark Twain's statement that it shouldn't be held against someone if they know more than one way to spell a word. Years later, at a conference on ADHD, a colleague said that Huck Finn had ADHD and would be treated today and have a better life. I said that the best that treatment could achieve would be to make him into a second-rate Becky Thatcher, and we should worry, at least a little, about that.

I had actually hoped that wild mushrooms might be helpful with my uncarefulness, that the stakes involved might have an alerting focusing effect.

First you have to be scanning for mushrooms as you walk along. If you're not looking for anything, maybe you won't see anything. If you look for mushrooms, maybe you'll see other things, but at least you're looking—I think that's what I thought—and then you find something mushroom-like. And here's where I thought the carefulness would come in: I would be picking and maybe eating something that would either taste incredibly good or would poison me.

I was so pleased with myself when I found what I thought were sweetbread mushrooms because they weren't all chewed up by insects the way so many of the edibles were and because there were so many of them, which meant maybe I'd be able to make wild mushrooms for a big group.

When I was gnawing on this nondescript piece of crap that was supposed to be bread-like and delicate, it didn't occur to me that I could have been wrong about the identity of the mushroom.

I was going to write the authors in question to tell them that the sweetbread mushroom had an indifferent taste and a disagreeable rubbery texture.

Fifteen minutes or so after eating the new mushroom, which I did not serve to my wife, thank God, my heart started racing, painful muscle spasms seized the back of my throat, and sweat started pouring off me. I remembered seeing a picture of a mushroom, one of the ones with a skull and crossbones under it, that was called the sweating mushroom. Funny name, I had thought.

"I think I might have made a mistake with the mushrooms," I said softly.

"What's that, dear?"

"I think I made a mistake with the mushrooms," I said too loudly, an octave above where I usually speak. Had I been sure I had ingested a less-than-fatal dose, I would have just gone quietly to bed, turned out the lights, and hoped for the best.

It didn't help that I was on the staff of the hospital where I went to get my stomach pumped. Had I been thinking more clearly, I would have gone elsewhere and maybe used another name.

"Doctor... what are you doing here?"

"I was hoping maybe you could start an IV, run some saline, and pump out my stomach."

"Why are you dripping sweat?"

"Funny you should notice that."

There are six ways mushrooms can be toxic. One or two would have been plenty. The less toxic ones make you very sick right away. With the ones that kill you, you feel fine for several days and then your liver dies and you follow shortly thereafter. Feeling sick as a dog and having sweat pour off me so soon after my mushroom meal was a good sign.

"At least it's not an *Amanita,*" I comforted myself.

What I had was muscarine poisoning, which shuts down the sympathetic nervous system, causing nausea, vomiting, diarrhea, painful constriction of the pharyngeal muscles, intense sweating, profuse tearing, and salivation—a relative bargain.

"I have a piece of the mushroom I ate and the Audubon guide to mushrooms open to the sweating mushroom right here." The sweetbread mushroom was right under it. "They look a lot alike, don't you think?"

My mind is like a lynch mob. If you know that about yourself, why on earth would you collect, cook, and eat wild mushrooms?

A few days after the *unfortunate incident,* for the first time in many months I was taking a walk without a basket or paper bag. I had promised my wife in a solemn manner that I would never never ever ever collect or eat wild mushrooms again.

On my return, walking into my own driveway, I couldn't believe it, but right behind the wall under the ash tree I saw a small patch of what could only be the sweetbread mushroom. Really.

My wife wasn't home. I took one of the mushrooms to make a spore print and hide it behind some books in my study. A few hours later I checked and it was pink, confirming that it was indeed the sweetbread mushroom. I didn't go back and pick them or eat the one I had picked. I plan to be back waiting at that spot next year, when my wife will be in a better mood.

I like to think of it not so much as a lack of carefulness as a wish to move forward.

I love finding out what happens next.

About the Author

Mark Vonnegut is the son of the late Kurt Vonnegut and Jane Cox Vonnegut and the author of *The Eden Express,* an ALA Notable Book. A full-time practicing pediatrician, he lives in Massachusetts with his wife and son.

10/10